It All Began With An EGG...

...And Hatched Into A Worldwide Industry

By Ken Klippen
Edited by Dean Hughson
Foreword by Art Papetti

Copyright 2006 by Ken Klippen
Printed in the United States. All rights reserved.

Library of Congress Control Number: 2006019028

ISBN 10-1-59872-469-X
ISBN 13-978-1-59872-469-1

Family Matters Books

A Division of L & L Publications
412 S. Davis • Hamilton, MO 64644 • 1-877-213-0812
www.familymattersbooks.com

Table of Contents

Acknowledgements 5
Lenny Ballas 7
Jerry Boatman 8
Brodhagen Family 9
Toby Catherman 12
Louis Dunckel 14
Cutler family 16
Bill Darr 19
Willem Enthoven 21
Morten Ernst 26
Torben Ernst 33
Clive Frampton 36
Jurgen Fuchs 38
Dan Gardner 39
Elliot Gibber 42
Joaquin Gomez Gomez 44
Brad Halpern 45
Mr. Wei Han 48
Mike Harris 57
Kit Henningsen 59
Vic Henningse 62
Edward F. Hoerning 64
Dean Hughson 67
Joanne Ivy 72
Bob Kellert 74
Connor Kennett, Jr. 75
Ken Klippen 77
Borge Korsgaard 81
Tim Luberski 82
Mike Luker 83
Don McNamara 86
Julian Madeley 88
Steve Manton 90

Roy Mosier	92
Greg Murch	93
Mr. Mac Ohi	99
Gregg Ostrander	100
Frank Pace	102
Arthur Papetti	105
Al Pope	110
Lou Raffel	111
Tom Rechsteiner	113
Dave Rettig	114
Goodwin (Goodie) Sonstegard	115
Rudolf "Rudy" O. Schmid	117
Phil Sonstegard	118
Bob Sparboe	120
Steve Stewart	123
Ilya Suster	124
Dennis Tyrrel	126
Filiep Van Bosstraeten	127
Dr. Milton G. Waldbaum	130
Hugh Wiebe	132
Vladimir Zacharius	134
Prologue by Arthur Papetti	135

Acknowledgements

This book would never have happened without the financial support of four key individuals; Arthur and Tony Papetti, Bill Darr, and Bob Sparboe. Although their stories are included in the biographies, these four had the vision and experience to know that "seed money" is essential in launching any new enterprise.

We want to thank all the industry leaders worldwide who responded to our questionnaire. Their stories are truly an inspiration to those who know them, and those who read of their accomplishments.

Special mention and a hearty thanks goes to Morten Ernst, who reached out to others worldwide to participate in the book, and to Mike Harris, who supplied many of the historical pictures showing where the egg products industry came from and where it is today.

We are indebted to the motivators in making this book a reality: Arthur Papetti, who dreamed the vision and encouraged its completion; Dean Hughson, who edited the stories and helped motivate people to participate, and Ken Klippen, who wrote the stories and injected his respect and admiration into their biographies for all who have participated.

This book is dedicated to all those leaders who helped shape the egg

Egg candling by hand, checking the interior contents prior to breaking. Today, automation has replaced scenes like this.

Closeup of modern egg breaking and separating of eggs.

products industry. We present the book also as a memorial to our departed egg friends who helped lead the way for many of us into this great industry.

Freight car being loaded with eggs outside of Seymour Poultry and Egg Plant in 1904.

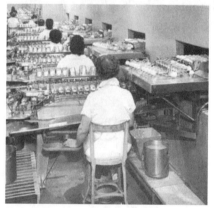

The speed and efficiency of modern egg breaking machines such as pictured above replaced the work crews of women who broke eggs at the processing plants.

The beginning of egg breaking as an industry started with this familiar site of the work crew of women hand breaking eggs.

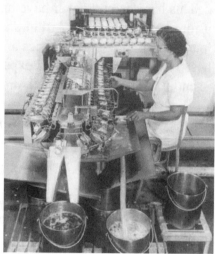

Egg breaking machine set to separate yolks from whites.

At the beginning of the 20th century, eggs for institutions were sold in cans.

Cases of eggs in storage, labeled and ready for shipment.

Lenny Ballas

Russia is famously known for its Faberge eggs and the egg displays at the Hermitage, the Winter Palace of the Russian Tsars. There are other good eggs coming from Russia and one that hatched into a leader in the U.S. egg products industry. Lenny Ballas has his family roots in Russia, but we consider him a "good egg" in America. Lenny's father, Max, immigrated to the U.S. from Russia in 1903. He worked with South Blick Egg Company in New York. Ballas Egg Company began in 1928 in Manhattan, New York City, and Lenny started working with the company in 1950. Lenny continued working and going to college, and graduated from Ohio State University in 1953 with a degree in Poultry Science. Craig Ballas, Lenny's son, also started working for the company. beginning in 1986. Lenny sold Ballas Egg Company to Wabash Valley Produce in Indiana 11 years ago and he and Craig have remained running the company.

Ballas Egg Company was originally a small butter/egg/bakery distribution company. A few years later, the company relocated to Zanesville, Ohio in 1940 and the original distribution center and warehouse in New York was sold in 1995 to Deb-El Foods.

Ballas Egg Company started off hand-breaking eggs until around 1945, when the company installed its first egg breaker. It's first egg dryer was installed in 1948 and Ballas Egg Company went on to patent the vacuum process for pasteurizing egg whites.

Max moved in 1976 to Lumber City, Georgia to start a farm for producing shell eggs. In 1990, Max Ballas died. Lenny lost his father and his mentor, but the training and experience Lenny gained helped him shape his company into an industry leader. Lenny has been active in many associations, including the original API group, UEP, American Egg Board, and was the second president of United Egg Association, representing the egg breakers.

In looking back, Lenny notes that products today are of higher quality before they are pasteurized than the old days when "Anything was broken." He's a strong advocate of breaking quality eggs, saying if you break "bad stuff" you get "bad product." With higher quality product, industry problems don't just go away. Lenny considers one of the problems that the U.S. egg products industry still has is access to Europe. He considers the difficulty in gaining access to Europe is largely a political problem.

Lenny has been one of the people that many egg men have looked up to over the years and has been a leader that all young people coming into the industry should emulate. Dean calls him an "eggman's eggman." To all of us, he's a "good egg".

Lenny has been married to Beatrice for 19 years and has 2 boys, 1 girl and 9 grandchildren.

Jerry Boatman

Jerry worked in quality control for Milton G. Waldbaum Company, Papettis of Iowa/Monark Egg, Sonstegard Foods, and now is with Sparboe Companies. He has been very fortunate to have had Dan Gardner and Arthur Papetti as mentors, and says he greatly benefited from his time with Bob Sparboe. This is none other than Jerry Boatman.

He become involved in the egg product industry more by need and chance then anything he had planned. Jerry had been living in New York City working for a marketing research company and he came to the realization he needed to get his degree. As he was driving across the country with his wife and 18-month-old daughter he remembered saying, "I think there is an egg plant in Wakefield. Maybe I can get a part time job while I finish my last two years of school." That conversation occurred in August 1970 and 35 years later he still has "yolk in my veins," he says.

Jerry received a BSE in Physical Science from Wayne State College and has been fortunate to grow with the industry and have experience in quality, production, procurement and sales.

After more than three decades in the business, Jerry said the upgrade of the egg quality with large laying complexes and in-line breakers were the biggest changes. The one thing that has not changed is

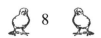

the continual over-production of shell eggs with prices not much different than they were 35 years ago. Jerry feels the industry will continue to be controlled by fewer people and it will become more and more a food business and not a commodity or farming business. Processing equipment will continue to improve, making processed eggs more like their freshly laid counterparts.

Jerry recalls his most memorable experience was his first visit to Japan and establishing a business relationship that is still in place almost 30 years later.

What would Jerry recommend for the incoming generation of egg people? Enjoy the ride because in a blink of an eye you will no longer be one of the young lions of the industry. It has been fun and as Bob Hope would say, "Thanks for the memories."

BRODHAGEN FAMILY

On May 24, 1948, at the age of 36, Frank Brodhagen Sr. purchased Northland Henneries in Abbotsford, Wisconsin. Located on Abbotsford's main street, Northland Henneries was an egg grading business. Northland Henneries was located in the heart of Abbotsford, very close to the railroad tracks and station. In fact, Northland Henneries' infrastructure was comprised of two old train cars–a passenger car and a coal car. The train cars had been pulled directly from the tracks behind and built together. Two additional floors were built on top of the cars.

Frank renamed the business Brodhagen's Northland Henneries. Frank continued to operate the business as a grading company. He focused much of his energy on grading and selling eggs into the Chicago market. A great deal of effort went into the egg route, which supplied his Chicago market. The egg route was made up of local and regional farmers and supermarkets. He would pick up small amounts of eggs from farms and grade them. The supermarkets would often have undergrades that Frank would use in combination with his to break. The breaking was done by hand, by four women, into tin cans. Obviously not pasteurized, the eggs reflected the standards of that time. When the egg route grew large enough, Frank had four ton and-a-half trucks out picking up eggs. Capitalizing on the fact that his trucks were making numerous stops – Frank decided to build small freezers onto each of the trucks. He then also began making ice cream and selling it at all of the egg route stops.

The front of the egg grading/breaking building was also utilized as a bakery. Frank and his three sons, Frank Jr., Jim, and Robert, would help Frank make frozen egg deliveries to the wholesale bakeries. They would then load the day old bakery goods into the truck and return it to the office to sell. It was extremely successful and very well-known. The boys clearly remember loading the bakery onto the truck as their father unloaded the frozen 30# tins into the bakery. In fact, many of the trips to the bakery were made with the boys sitting on tin cans in the front, seeing as how there was not a passenger seat for them to sit on. Frank Sr., would tell them to hold onto the dashboard.

In 1968, Frank put in his first egg breaker: A 12 case/hr Seymour. He and his wife earned a trip to Florida for buying the Seymour. Frank also changed the name to Abbotsford Produce Egg Products.

In the early 70's, Frank discontinued his egg routes. Instead, his boys, now old enough to drive, were picking up eggs at larger regional producers such as Luoma Egg Ranch and Hixton Egg Company. Jim, second oldest, remembers returning from Hixton Egg Co. and getting pulled over by a state trooper. When asking why he was being pulled over, the officer commented that he "didn't like the way things looked."

Jim agreed, "The truck was a wreck."

In 1971, with the inception of the Egg Inspection Act, the USDA had many more requirements that the current location could not accommodate. So, needing to borrow money, Frank contacted the governor – who helped him borrow the money to build an egg processing facility on the other side of town.

Frank purchased 14 acres of land on Abbotsford's east side and built his egg processing plant. An egg cooler was planned for shell eggs – that actually was a restaurant for many years.

Frank Jr. , James and Robert remember that although the plant was new – it wasn't that technologically advanced. There were no pumps to pump the liquid egg from one area to another. So, bucket by bucket they would transfer liquid egg. Robert commented that you would become so hypnotized by moving these buckets over and over again that once in awhile, a bucket of yolk accidentally got put into the egg whites. Additionally, there were no pallets for moving pails around. Instead, the boys would often form a human conveyor and pass the buckets from one to the other. Once in awhile they could talk their friends into helping out, to speed things along. Loading and unloading trucks was a very labor-intensive and time-consuming event. The egg products were often loaded onto the trucks very late at night to ensure that they would remain frozen or cool. This way their dad could make the deliveries early in the morning to the customer. The egg shells were loaded into metal garbage cans that the boys would then have to take to the dump–rain, shine or freezing. There were many, many late nights and early mornings for the teenage boys.

As the business continued to grow and the needs for liquid and frozen egg products increased, plant improvements were made. Pasteurization, pumps and numerous other improvements took place. In 1980 a new egg breaker replaced the first breaker. The company continued to grow as a commodity egg product supplier. In 1989 the second Seymour egg breaker went in.

The three boys continued to operate the egg processing business

through the 80s and 90s.

In 2002, the company entered into a new phase of business. The third generation of Brodhagens, Kathy and Eric, also joined the company. Becoming a specialty egg breaking and packaging company was the new niche for the company. The Brodhagens doubled the size of the plant to include extended shelf life egg processing for grocery stores and food service. This has been a very successful venture for Abbotsford Produce. The company continues to focus on the specialties processing demands and continues to anticipate growth and strategic product development

Today, you will see all three generations of Brodhagens at the office, every day of the week. Frank, now 94, continues to join his sons and two grandkids at the office.

TOBY CATHERMAN

At meetings of industry associations, he's quiet and reflective, but when he speaks, his words do not hold back the power and punch of his convictions. He believes strongly and acts strongly. He's a strong advocate that any industry should lead and not follow, and he has demonstrated this form of leadership through his chairmanship of United Egg Association (UEA) and in his position with Michael Foods in Quakertown, Pennsylvania. Taking the reins of that association, Toby Catherman helped foster a strong working relationship with the federal agencies in Washington, D.C. USDA's Food Safety and Inspection Service came to appreciate the strength of UEA in presenting a united front on issues and in working to develop the industry's food safety perspective. He hopes this will continue in the future.
His company has also participated as members of United Egg Producers (UEP) with Terry Baker and Tim Beebe of Michael Foods, Inc. serving on its board of directors. Although Toby credits UEP with being a significant factor in developing the role of the industry today, he feels that it has developed too much into a "political boy's club" for a very few and it needs to re-sharpen its goals. Every member of UEP should benefit from its direction, and the policies of UEP should reflect these benefits to all its members. UEA, he says on the other hand, is subject

and purpose-driven, but he wants to see it fully develop into a powerful organization utilizing its membership brain-trust.

Where did this man come from? After getting a BS degree in business management from Kurtztown State College, he started working as an assistant controller at Weis Markets. He was here for about 2-1/2 years when the Quaker State Farms management and Cooper Lybrand (who were auditing Weis at the time) asked him to be their controller. That was 1978 when he was 25 years old. The next 27 years, Toby stayed in one place; however his position changed repeatedly due to the company's first being acquired by Papetti's Hygrade Egg Products, and finally, Michael Foods, Inc. He now serves in the procurement capacity for Michael Foods. His skills in auditing, coupled with his industry knowledge, has led Toby to understand the potential for every egg products plant and the managers who operate those plants. He jests when recommending to the new generation of egg industry people to first get involved in industry matters early. But first, he says, learn every aspect of the business, pack eggs, unload a truck, make feed, run a pasteurizer, prepare a business plan and market it to a customer. Then, says Toby "watch your efforts blossom for 60 seconds and start again." It's tenacity like this that shapes leaders to pick yourself up and move forward when circumstances knock you down. And that will happen from time to time.

Over the years, Toby has seen volumes of processed egg products expand at phenomenal rates, especially at Michael Foods, and has watched as industry consolidations have occurred. He expects this process to not only continue, but to speed up until there are only ten major players with some minor, small family regional companies. He also appreciates how the shell egg industry and egg products industry have developed specialty products to expand market share and capture more of the consumer dollar.

What changes need to develop in the egg products? He says to market globally shelf-stable liquid.

Toby commented on how he enjoyed the last few decades of long hours and hard work. He commented on the people who helped shape the industry and his views. The most memorable experience for Toby was having the opportunity to work with people like Arthur Papetti and Terry Baker. While Terry is with the same firm, he is located in Nebraska and Toby in Pennsylvania. They share their thoughts, ideas, and complaints daily with each other, and this helped shape a partnership/friendship that will endure. He recognizes and applauds Arthur Papetti's God-given ability to create a trusting environment, allowing the nurturing and mentoring of one's abilities and ambitions. His leadership today in the egg products industry is helping others to nurture and mentor their abilities and ambitions. Just watch him when he's quiet and reflective, but then stand back and watch when he speaks his convictions. The power and punch of those moments will strengthen the ambition of anyone who seeks to be a leader.

Toby is married to Ellen for nearly 30 years now, and has two children–Kristin, who works at the admissions department for Elizabethtown College, and Katie, who is a student in Pharmacy at Wilkes University.

LOUIS DUNCKEL

Louis Dunckel was in his 60s when he decided to change careers by developing a pre-cooked scrambled egg mix and diced eggs. That is the way with innovators in the egg products industry. They have a good idea and follow through in its development.

Louis was born and raised on a dairy farm originally settled by his great, great, great, grandfather. To complete a project needed for an FFA award, he got 500 hens – raised them – laid them, completed the project and got the award.

Apparently the poultry bug bit him and the poultry farm grew and grew. In the 1980s, with his family, he operated Preston Egg, Inc., with 420,000 layers and 120,000 growing pullets. He may have been among the first in New York State to offer Grade AA on cartons at retail.

During the 1970s with his son, David, and son-in-law, Gary, he operated a dairy farm with 250 registered Holsteins. The poultry manure from the egg farm was utilized as an excellent fertilizer.

In 1988, at age 64, he changed careers. Working with the advice of Dr. Robert Baker of Cornell University, he developed a process for making pre-cooked scrambled eggs and diced eggs – called "Tray Ready Scrambled Eggs" and "Salad Ready Diced Eggs." He experimented with a very old steam cooker in the kitchen at home. This was from a man who didn't know how to boil water and, if left alone for a meal, ate crackers and milk, reported his wife, Helen.

From these experiments, Egg Low Farms, Inc. was born. The product was about ten years ahead of its time. Today people are looking for prepared foods with the ease of this product. Louis died in 1993 of cancer before ever knowing for sure that it was a success. His wife, Helen, and son, David, continued to operate the business until the present.

No additives (except Citric Acid to retain the color) are added to the product which gives it an excellent flavor and consistency. The eggs are not rubbery or chewy. The product is made for institution and restaurant use.

During this time, eggs got a very bad name as being too high in cholesterol. Since that time, this has been shown to be a false report. One of his products was with added egg white to lower the cholesterol, but still have a good, tasty product. There was a little demand at the time, but not the amount he felt was possible. Since that time, the New York City School System has added the "Tray Ready Scrambled Egg with Added Egg White" to their menu in an effort to give the students a more wholesome menu. *Story written by Helen Dunckel.*

Louis D. Dunckel
196 Dunckel Road
Oxford, NY 13830
Born:10/5/1923. Died 1993
Married: 9/2/1946; wife Helen
3 children: Barbara, Betty and David

Cutler family

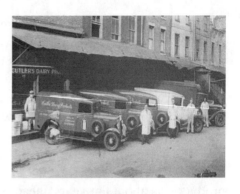

The Cutler family has a long history in the egg industry. Hyman Cutler began a retail and egg business in London in 1892 after he immigrated from Czarist Russia. Six years later, he moved to the U.S. and took up residence selling butter and eggs from his horse and wagon in Philadelphia, Pennsylvania. He lived above the store with his wife and five children (two sons and 3 daughters). In 1922 Hyman brought into the business Charles Chalotnick, who married into the family and took the name of Cutler as his surname.

In 1928 Hyman died and Charles took as a partner his brother-in-law, Abraham. The business expanded into manufacturing under a new name, "Cutler's Tasty Sour Cream," in addition to eggs. The other brothers-in-law, Bernard and Edward, came into the business in 1940. A year later they started drying eggs by hand with a

milk dryer producing powdered eggs at 200 lbs. per hour. Their only customer was the U.S. government which bought for the armed forces in WWII. That dryer operated 24 hours per day, seven days per week.

Charles died in 1945, and with the end of the war, the dryer was dismantled. The business returned to fresh liquid eggs. Edward passed away in 1946, yet his wife, Ray, entered the business as the finance officer. Charles' son, Leonard, and Edward's son, Coleman, returned from serving in the military in 1946 to enter into the family business. They expanded into frozen egg products. The business did well and they expanded into dairy plants in Staunton, Virginia and Millsboro, Delaware. Cutler's also had hand breaking egg operations in Colfax, Iowa; Bridgewater, Virginia; Pittsburgh, Pennsylvania; and Baltimore, Maryland.

Harold Cutler (Abraham's son) joined the business in 1958, followed by Joel Cutler (Bernard's son) two years later when he finished college. Cutler's opened another egg breaking plant in December 1971 in Abbeville, Alabama with a full line of frozen and dried egg products. Harold moved his family to Alabama in June of 1972, joined later by Joel and his family. Harold's two sons, Jeffrey and Alan, entered the business after college.

Coleman's two sons; Edward and Larry, joined the Philadelphia operation after college. In all, three generations of Cutlers worked together for 20 years until they sold in 2001. Jeff and Harold still work in Alabama, while Edward and Larry are in the Philadelphia plant. At the time of the sale, the Cutlers were breaking 5,000 cases per day in Philadelphia while Alabama was breaking 8,000 cases per day. Their accounts included Tasty Cake, Entenmanns, Kelloggs, Campbell's Soup, and others.

Leonard recalls the most significant change in the industry occurred when the egg products law began in 1970. Having all egg products pasteurized and under federal inspection improved the quality of egg products and reduced the number of operations around the country. Cutler's was among the first to start pasteurizing before the law was passed.

Coleman says November 22, 1962 was the most significant day for him as they installed their first Seymour breaking machine at 20 cases per hour (that day was also famous as then President John Kennedy was shot in Dallas, Texas).The new machine took the place of ten employees and revolutionized the industry.

Joel Cutler started in our family egg business while attending Temple University in Philadelphia in the 60s with a major in electrical engineering. Joel put his education to use after college. He invented and patented the first egg and ingredient batching system that produced a consistent product mix. Years later, he assisted in inventing an extended shelf life liquid egg product. Joel also designed and installed at all three Cutler plants all of the process control systems, having designed, programmed and installed over fifteen industrial control computers.

Joel's engineering background helped him develop an appreciation for new technologies. But he credits the most significant invention was the egg breaking machine. When Joel first started in the business, all eggs were broken by hand. One of his first jobs was to break the eggs in this manner. A very good person could break and separate 4-6 cases/hr. Naturally it was difficult to keep up those averages all day long. Joel had a few ideas about a breaking machine, but Seymour Foods came out with the #101 first. Cutler's installed their first machines in November of 1963. The other big change that greatly affected Cutler's was in 1971 with the mandatory inspection by the USDA. Joel noted that this mandatory law made the playing field equal between all companies and brought up the sanitary and physical standards of the industry.

When asked what Joel would do differently, if he could roll back the clock, " I would do it all over again it, in much the same way," he said. He would have liked to have played an even greater role in the International Egg Commission, rising to the office of Vice Chairman of the Egg Processors International.

Joel predicts the industry will continue to grow with even more consolidation in the future. He feels the industry will see even faster egg breaking machines and electronics playing an even bigger role in the production and processing areas. This will lead to breaking machines that do the entire job of the operator better and faster.

Joel's most memorable experience in this industry is serving on the UEA Technical Committee and working on and developing the standards used in the new Egg Pasteurization manual that is being used all over the world.

Joel listed three persons who he felt had the greatest impact on his life in the egg products industry: Art Papetti, Vic Hennigsen, Dan Gardner. And the associations having the biggest impact: The American Egg Board with their sponsorship of the Egg Nutrition Center, which played an extremely important role in overcoming the bad publicity about eggs; the UEA, which brought most of the industry together and has been a major reason for the success of the industry by fighting everything from USDA issues, to animal right issues, to export issues.

What does Joel hope to be doing 5 -10 years from now. "Easy," he said, "Playing golf."

BILL DARR, founder of American Dehydrated Foods, Inc. (ADF), International Dehydrated Foods, Inc.(IDF), and co-founder of Food Ingredients Technology Company, LLC (FITCO).

What do egg processors do with their spinnings (the membrane-trapped egg white left over in broken eggs)? Landfills will often take the dry shells, but don't want the liquid. Many egg processors and egg producers alike have truly benefitted from Bill Darr's plan to add value to what many consider a waste product. Bill truly is an entrepreneur pioneer and a gentleman. Anyone who meets Bill Darr of ADF-fame understands and agrees with that description.

Bill created a new company in 1978 that today processes millions of pounds of inedible egg into a powder for pet food companies sold throughout the world. The production of dehydrated eggs by ADF, Inc. expanded into other meat and poultry products for pet foods. ADF,

Inc. has production facilities in Missouri, Alabama and Georgia. In 1982, Bill founded IDF, Inc. located in Monett, Missouri and produces mechanically separated chicken, dehydrated chicken, turkey and beef products. In 1990 Bill co-founded FITCO, LLC located in Anniston, Alabama and manufactures dehydrated chicken, chicken fat and broth. Bill first got involved in the egg industry in 1956 when he was a junior at Southwest Missouri State University in Springfield, MO. His part-time work at Henningsen Foods opened up full-time opportunities at Henningsen, including quality control manager, director of technical services and general production manager. In 1974 he left Missouri for Mississippi to serve as the president of Pets And Such. That four year experience was the springboard for his venture into processing inedible egg into pet food ingredients.

Bill's plan was to collect the broken eggs from packing stations and inedible liquid in tankers from processing plants and spray-dry the liquid into a powder. The premium pet food companies recognized the high quality protein value from egg (the higher the quality, the less protein needed to provide the essential amino acids). The egg also added Choline, an essential element for brain function.

Over the years, Bill watched the consolidations in the egg production and processing industries, the movement from small flocks to mega-producers, and the growth in egg breaking by processors. Bill recalls when egg breaking was only 10% of the total egg production supplies to where today it is reaching for 40% of the total. The positives to this growth are increased sophistication and much improved egg quality.

Some of the memorable persons who had a direct impact on Bill's career in the egg industry are Vic Henningsen, Sr., Dr. Harry Slosberg, and Dr. Richard Forsythe.

Bill is married to Virginia and has two daughters, Marsha Slaight and Sheri Hellweg. In his business he has two sons-in-law; Tom Slaight, Chairman of the Board, and Kurt Hellweg, President and CEO. He also boasts about his four grandchildren and two step grandchildren.

Bill's hopes for the future are the next generation of egg people who will be able to flatten the peaks and valleys of egg production by creating new innovative egg products. We are hoping with you, Bill.

WILLEM ENTHOVEN

NIVE Holland

Willem Enthoven worked from 1949 - 1973 in the family business, D. Enthoven & Sons, and served as the managing director of NIVE, one of the leading egg products companies in Holland, from 1973-1985. He continued serving on the board and representing NIVE at meetings in Holland and abroad until officially resigning from all duties in 1995. His story provides insight into the growth of the egg industry in Holland and how the Common Agricultural Policy (CAP) applied to eggs and exports.

Willem's grandfather started farming in 1885, near where Schiphol Airport is now located, breeding and raising chickens for shell eggs. He sold them from door to door in the neighborhood. When his three sons entered, they expanded the business. In the beginning of last century they sold more eggs than they could produce. Thus, the egg trading company of D. Enthoven & Sons was founded and the egg production and packing plant stopped. Around 1910, they entered into the export business, first to UK and after 1918, also to Germany. When war broke out in 1940, the company was one of the leading firms in Holland trading and exporting eggs. In 1945, at the end of the war, shell egg production in Holland was reduced to about 10-15% of pre-war levels. Egg consumption was rationed and sales were directed by government through selected egg packing stations, the family company being one of them. Food manufacturing companies (mayonnaise manufacturers, bakeries, etc.) also could buy shell eggs for industrial use through the rationing system. While the mayonnaise manufacturers only wanted egg yolk and the bakeries wanted egg white, the company was asked if they were willing to do the breaking and separating. So the eggs products industry started as an additional activity of egg packing. Yearly increases of egg production after the end of the war were small, due to the lack of foreign currency to buy overseas feedstuffs. In addition, the government regulated sales both nationally and internationally. In the 1950s the government made sale contracts to UK. Sales to Germany were based on the quantity shipped in the UK permits. Enthoven remembers that shortly after joining the family business he found out that the combination of sales to the UK and Germany was only valid for fresh shell eggs and not for preserved eggs. In their plant they had the capacity for storing eggs in lime water. Willem stored about 5000 eggs and sold then to an advocate manufacturer in Germany. The profit per egg made on this transaction Enthoven has never made again in all his years in the egg trade.

Willem was born in 1925 and lived all his life near the packing station. He grew up in the business helping sort, candle and pack eggs. After finishing his studies in economics at the University of Rotterdam in 1949, he entered as the youngest grandchild in the family business, joining four other family members already working there.

In the 1950s egg production in Holland started to increase rapidly. This was partly due to the support and protection from the government. Small farmers, at that time, represented a large political vote. Egg production gave the producer a daily income. To protect and stimulate the smaller farmers in certain relatively poor regions, egg production was reserved for these small farms. Toward the end of the 1950s no egg producer in Holland was allowed to own more than 700 hens. This law has been of great impact on the Dutch egg industry. Contrary to development in other European countries where large egg production farms were started, egg production in Holland has, for a long time, remained a family business.

In view of political interest for small farmers, the poultry industry was one of the first sectors where the government stimulated a new structure for organizations of producers, trade and industry in commodity boards. With a background in judicial and economic knowledge, Willem soon was elected to the committee's advising government. Right from the beginning Willem became a board member for egg products in the Dutch Eggs Packers Association.

What were some of the changes that Willem saw over the five decades in the egg business? In the 1960s shell egg production was increasing rapidly due to new production systems (cage production, and through genetics with increasing egg production per hen). In certain countries (UK, South Africa, Australia, Canada, Israel) marketing boards were set up to regulate the market. That meant guaranteeing the producer a minimum price and removing surplus eggs. Faced with the impossibility of selling these eggs on the world market, transforming these surpluses into egg products became the policy. So new production capacity was created, not founded on the market for egg products, but on a surplus situation in worldwide egg production. Since it was not founded on economic principles, it soon created an over-supply of processed eggs. It became clear that this was no solution and that it could not be the basis for a profit-making industry. The responsibility for buying the raw material and selling the processed product came back to the individual manufacturer. For some, the changeover from working under the umbrella of a marketing board system to free enterprise was too difficult and they quit the industry.

What does Willem see for the future of the industry? Egg consumption per capita in the form of shell eggs will decrease, egg consumption in processed form will increase.

What is the most memorable experience for Willem? In the 1960s, German sausage manufacturers were using frozen egg whites as binding agent in their products. For whatever reason, this stopped suddenly. The egg products industry, especially in Germany and Holland where most of the separating was done, was faced with a surplus situation. Sales were possible to Japan, but prices on that market were too low for European industry. After discussion with the authorities of the European Commission in Brussels, it was understood that the Commission was willing to increase the export subsidy for this item to the Far East on the condition that it was a one-time transaction supported by the European industry as a whole. A consortium of leading egg whites producers in Germany and Holland was formed with Sander de Fluiter

(NIVE) as coordinator and a large contract with Japan was made. Good personal contacts between industry leaders in Europe and with the industry and their government representatives in Brussels made the successful realization of this common contract possible.

In looking at the role of associations, Willem noted the Dutch contributions. From 1956, after signing the Treaty of Rome by Germany, France, Italy, Holland, Belgium and Luxemburg, it was apparent that the future founding of the European Economic Community with their proposed Common Agricultural Policy would have an enormous impact on the poultry industry, not only for the six member countries, but also for the rest of Western Europe and countries like Poland Scandinavia, South Africa, Australia and China, that were active on the European markets. From the beginning it was clear that the European Commission would not seek the advice of national organizations, but only would consult communal organizations that would speak for the EEC industry as a whole.

In 1958 – 1960 contacts between national organizations to come to a European Forum began. Through the Dutch organization, Willem was, from the start, actively engaged with these international contacts. In 1960 the European Union of Trade Associations of Eggs, Egg Products and Poultry was formed. Although at that moment the egg products industry in Europe was relatively unimportant, it now had input through the Union contact with the policymakers in Brussels. Implanting the Common Agricultural Policy into regulations for different agricultural sectors was an enormous task. For the animal sector the overall structure of that policy was a system of levies and sluice gate prices (prices for imports from third countries which were earmarked as dumping prices) as a basis for supplementary levies. For exports there was a system of subsidies and for some countries or group of countries, supplementary subsidies. The basis of this system of levies and subsidies is mainly the price difference for grain in and outside the EEC market. For products like eggs and poultry meat which used feed grains for their production levies, it had to be calculated on their grain component. For processed products like egg products, further calculations had to be made on basis of the levy for shell eggs. Knowledge on technical details, for example, how many shell eggs are necessary to produce 1 kilo of egg yolk and or whites, was then necessary. The European Commission lacked the technical and practical knowledge, especially of these further processed products of a relatively new and small industry. Willem was asked – indirectly - by Mr. Mansholt, Agricultural Commissioner in the European Commission, to assist and advise his staff by making concepts for these calculations. For example, based on a levy of x for a kilo of shell eggs what must be the levy of 1 kilo of egg yolk and 1 kilo of egg white? A formula had to be used for this, taking into account what is under practical processing conditions the weight component for yolk and white, but also what is under normal market conditions the relative value of 1 kilo yolk and 1 kilo white (if only the weight component would be considered levies on whites would be too high in relation to their price and yolk too low). For dried products, further components as water content and loss during processing had to be incorporated. For the international trade in egg products the outcome of these calculations resulting in levies for imports and subsidies for exports would be of vital interest. To be on a voluntary basis in close contact with the concept making of these new market regulations, to try and implement what is practical and technically possible, was very interesting. Willem found it certainly helpful in understanding the problems in the much criticized Common Agricultural Policy with its complicated marketing regulations.

In 1962 at a Poultry Conference in Australia the idea for an international organization was conceived and discussed. At the Second International Egg Marketing Conference in Italy in 1964 the International Egg Commission (IEC) was founded. One of their terms of reference would be to examine the possibility of standardizing the quality of eggs and eggs products on an international basis. As a result a Subcommittee on the Standardization of Eggs Products was formed comprised entirely of specialists and with Mr. Konings (secretary of European Union) as Honorary Secretary. Willem was asked by the Executive Committee of IEC to chair this subcommittee. In 1966 the committee submitted a draft and at the Warsaw Conference the IEC Council accepted it as "Standardization of Egg Products" and published it.
Then in the European Union occupied itself with a concept for the Standardization of Egg Products. Because of the close personal contacts between IEC and the Union (the Chairman and Secretary of their eggs products committees were identical) the proposals accepted by the IEC

and those submitted by the Union to the authorities of the EEC were fundamentally the same. The harmonization of these sets of proposals on a global and European level has helped with their general acceptance.

Originally started with six countries in 1970s, more countries have joined the EEC. The basis of the economic community is free internal trade between member's countries. Only in matters of health care does each member has its own national responsibility. Sometimes, members banned imports for veterinary reasons to help their own industry. In the interest of international trade, harmonization of veterinary regulations was necessary. After many discussions and consultations with the industry in 1989 the European Commission published "Directive for Hygienic and Health Questions for Production and Trade in Egg Products," regulating all the veterinary aspects in national and international trade.

MORTEN ERNST

Many industry leaders are well traveled, having visited processing facilities in other countries, but how many people in the egg industry can claim one full year flying (more than 8,000 hours) visiting egg people around the world?

Morten Ernst can make that claim, having crossed the Atlantic more than 360 times, Europe to Asia nearly 100 times, and the Pacific to Asia at more than 100 times. Morten has logged in more than 3 million miles visiting the industry in North and South America, East and Western Europe, Africa and Asia. His first trip to South America, which led to the first modern egg products factory in Argentina and two in Brazil, was made in 1974. His first trip to Japan was in 1978, and to India in 1993, where he became a partner in the first egg products plant there. He first went to China in 1984, and in 1997 he became the first foreign partner in an egg products plant in that country since the early 1900s (he entered into his second partnership in 2001). The Joint Venture Agreement to become partner in the first China plant in 1997 was signed at his hospital bed in Copenhagen. Morten had experienced a blood clot in one leg from sitting too much in airplanes (this was the official cause). It went into his lung, and after his hospitalization he was told he was very lucky to have survived. This happened during a heavy travel schedule in the U.S., visiting installations with his future Chinese partner and his delegation. If there is anyone more traveled in the egg industry than Morten, we don't know it.

But how did he start this business of traveling and conducting business with egg people on five continents? Having finished his business education, Morten Ernst longed to get out and see the world. He recalled during his apprentice period in Odense, Denmark – at the age of 16 or 17 – during the summers at lunch break, he would walk over to the highway nearby, sit in the grass on the side and eat his lunch while looking at the passing cars going east or west. Morten's home town was located in the middle of Denmark, and going east or west meant having to pass through Odense. His lunch spot therefore was ideally located as a watching spot. He would see many cars with foreign registration plates, from Germany, England, France, Italy, etc., and in his mind he would be in Germany, England or France. It was a tough task to be in all these countries in only half an hour, and getting back to reality often meant a scolding from his boss when he caught Morten returning back to work late.

After his apprentice period he landed his first job at a large grocery wholesale import company in Copenhagen. He worked in the shipping department, which meant doing all the import documents, going to the port and getting the ships' cargoes cleared through customs, and later on, he also did cargo inspection for damage, etc. This further whetted Morten's appetite for seeing the world . . . all these ships coming from far away, with raisins from California, rice from Asia, nuts from South America or paper from Finland. This was almost too much for a young man to handle, and after two years of "torture," he finally just had to get out into the world.

Morten was fortunate to have grown up in an international home . . . not just any international home, but an international EGG home. His father started in the egg business in 1942, three years before Morten was born, so his whole childhood was filled with stories about other countries, and as his father was a great believer in personal relationships with suppliers and customers alike, many foreigners visited their home. Often

they were treated to home-cooked dinners where Morten's brother and he often were allowed to join . . . not understanding what was spoken, but fascinated by it nevertheless. So, as Morten's shipping career did not seem to hold any international challenges for him, he asked his father if he could go to one of his egg products factories somewhere to better his language skills. After two years in Copenhagen, 22 years old, already married and with one child, he got his big break! In the summer of 1967 Morten said goodbye to Copenhagen and hello to London, England to work at Londegg, which was a partnership between Sanovo and S. Behr Mathews. Mr. Ilya Suster was in charge of S. Behr & Mathews, and he was waiting for Morten and his wife at Liverpool Street Station, together with Morten's father's partner and close friend, Vagn Holck Andersen. They had arranged for them to live in a rented room at an address near the factory. Morten recalls the weekly rent was 5 UK£. His first job in the egg industry was to learn pasteurizing of eggs at Londegg, later also drying, as well as regular office work. Morten's wife, Pipper, studied English at the Pitmann's School of English while Morten worked at the factory before moving on to Sanovo's egg products company in Germany. Here Morten started working first in the administration, which was located in the old Freihafen (Freeport) of Hamburg, later on in the factory near Bremen. Having finished the "basics," it was natural for him to accept a job at the head office back in Denmark. Here Morten worked in the export department of Lactosan, which was the largest egg products processor in Scandinavia. Later on he also got to work for Sanovo Engineering. One of his first responsibilities was to exhibit the Sanovo Egg Breaking machine outside of Denmark for the first time. This was in Brno in Czechoslovakia in September 1968, at the same time when the Russians invaded the country. In the shadow of Russian tanks and soldiers patrolling the streets, this exhibit became the turn-around point for the Sanovo egg breaking machine, and a jump start to future successes for the company. In late 1969 Morten was offered the great chance to move to New York to set up Sanovo's newly established company there. At this point he felt he was finally out in the world, and except for a couple of years in the mid-seventies, he never moved back to Denmark.

In his formative years - from 1962 to 1965, Morten was an apprentice in a grocery wholesale company in his hometown of Odense in Denmark. This taught him much about foods and logistics. He worked in the office, as well as executing orders to the supermarkets and groceries, of which at that time there were at least one in every small town and many more in the cities. He went on many a trip to deliver foods, canned goods, sugar and flour to these groceries and bakeries throughout the island on which Odense is the capital. In the evening he went to business school. This continued after his "graduation" in Copenhagen when he got a job in the shipping department of the largest grocery wholesale importer in Scandinavia. This company was made up by most of the grocery chains in Denmark. Here his job was to handle all import formalities of all the foreign goods sold by the groceries and supermarkets. It was a very good education for a young man at that time, as he learned about international logistics, documentation, etc. This lasted two years to 1967, when he went through training in the egg products business in England, Germany and Denmark before he started his "real" egg career in the U.S. in late 1969.

Morten's father Torben started his egg career in 1942 at the age of 24 as the first employee at what later became the Lactosan/Sanovo group. The egg products business was his world until he passed away in 2003. He was active in this business for 60 years! He was a great person to learn from. All who remember him will agree that he was a true gentleman in the old sense when a person's word was his bond. He was one of the European pioneers in the business, and one of the first to expand processing across borders. Morten worked with his father in Lactosan-Sanovo for 20 years until Torben's retirement in 1986. At that time, Morten established his own company, Ovotec, and when Torben joined him a year later they worked together for an additional 16 years. Both he and Morten were fortunate to also work in the egg business with Morten's son, Christoffer. Upon graduation from Towson University in Maryland in 1999, Christoffer wanted to "get his hands dirty" before starting his MBA. At that time Morten had just started making egg powder in a joint venture in Central China, and Christoffer was quick to jump on the chance to go to China. He got some preliminary training in a couple of egg products factories in the U.S,, and off he went to work in Central China near the ancient city of Xian. He worked in the factory there, and later joined Morten's company in Shanghai where he became Chief Representative until he joined Sanovo Engineering as head of their company in China. Morten's daughter Pernille is married and lives in Washington, DC. She worked as the company secretary at Ovotec in Denmark for eight years, so for several years they were three generations and four family members working together.

When Morten started in the egg products business, trade across borders was done by few players, and import regulations were less complicated.

The European egg products processors were export champions primarily
due to the logistics factor, as much of the international business was done between countries inside Europe. A handful of European companies exported overseas to Canada, the US and South America, as well as to a few destinations in the Far East, primarily Japan. The rule was to keep good personal relations with customers, and when there were problems these were mostly worked out in a gentlemanly manner. Today, when the world is supposed to give everybody access to everybody's market, there are numerous import regulations that, in fact, have made exports more difficult. Some large markets are almost completely closed for imports today, while others use any minor excuse to close doors temporarily if they need to protect their local industry. Morten believes that protectionism has increased under the cover of quality, and this will force former exporters to stop exporting to certain markets, or to establish themselves in the markets where they want to sell products. This, in fact, is how the industry will become more and more global.

In looking at the progress made in the egg products industry, Morten says that "value-added egg products" was a major contributor to the surge in egg processing. Led by Japan, pasteurized, processed egg products are at 40+ percent of egg consumption in some countries. From an industry point of view, Morten would like to see more research being done, and he would like to see the industry viewed more as a member of the food industry, rather than merely a bulk supplier of an ingredient. As it is now, processors basically pass on much of the added value to the food processor. "That's not good" says Morten. He also thinks that the industry must be better at dealing with the animal rights issues, and the ever increasing importance of lobbying the politicians.

Would Morten do it all over again? He says that his wife might not agree with him, but yes, he would do it all over again. He said it has been a very busy life with so much traveling and meeting so many interesting people around the world. He has had so many wild experiences, from geese hunting far away in the Siberian tundra to Jaguar hunting deep in the Central American jungle, and the occasional emergency landing (one at the highest located commercial airport in the world, on top of the Andes in Ecuador). The downside was not being at home much when the children were growing up. He credits his ability to conduct international business to his understanding wife, who took care of the home and the bringing up of the children. The upside is an internationally oriented family at ease in a local, global world. His father's "internationalization" of his kids has resulted in a family now living in Denmark, Belgium, Switzerland, USA, China, England and France.

The egg industry has blessed Morten and his family with many friends, and he is happy to say that he has friends in the industry from his father's era as well as from his son's. The egg industry has both grown in size and at the same time gotten smaller in terms of numbers of companies. The International Egg Commission is a good example of the industry having grown from a small family to a large one - three generations actually, just like his own.

What would Morten change, if he could? The supply and demand situation is what he would change because, from his perspective, the industry has never understood how to get the production in line with the demand.

What does the future hold? When the egg industry makes money, it spends it on flock expansion. When the market falls because of too many eggs, it reduces the flock size. This is nothing new, but Morten notes it will push the weaker players out of the market or into the arms of the stronger ones. The move towards fewer, but larger macro companies with strong financial clout is what Morten expects in the future. The larger companies will have the funds for research, and they will be ahead of consumers in knowing the trends. He foresees these mega companies having mega processing plants operated by computers and "technobrains." Some will become divisions of multi-food processors as these conglomerates move towards vertically-integrated, global macro operations. The industry already is in the consolidation phase and will finally become truly global.

Morten's first IEC meeting was in Madrid, Spain in 1970, which was also his first full year living in the U.S. (he spent 15 years of his "egg life" in the U.S., 18 years in Europe, and so far, five in Asia). This gave him the opportunity to arrange a trip to Europe where many old-timer U.S. egg processors joined. Being European gave him an opportunity to "bond" with many of the great names in the industry, such as Dan Gardner, Glen Olson, Goodie Sonstegard, Mike Meloro, Frank Santo, all of them being introduced to the IEC for the first time. Morten was only 25 at the time, while all these industry giants, of course, were much older and wiser. It gave him the opportunity to get to know all these egg people early on, and benefitted him and his business throughout his 15 years in the U.S. and beyond. Today Morten serves as IEC's Ambassador in Asia.

Of the many great people in the industry, there is one person who stands out in Morten's mind as truly outstanding. His name is Vagn Holck Andersen, a well known and respected Danish business personality. Vagn was the co-founder of Sanovo in 1961 and immediately became a valuable, key person in shaping the future of the company, together with his father. In the process, they became indispensable friends. In the mid-1960s Vagn left Sanovo when he was offered an opportunity outside the industry. This career path opened up to him many top posts in Denmark, of which the most notable perhaps was president and later chairman of Lego, the famous Danish toy company. Morten had known Vagn and his family as a boy, and as a young man during his brief stay in Copenhagen he helped Morten on weekends with his business school economics. In 1969 when Vagn and his father had set up Sanovo USA in New York, it was Vagn who proposed that Morten run that company. Morten's father thought he was too young, but Vagn insisted that Morten would be the right person for the job. Morten clearly remembers that he followed him to the gate in Copenhagen airport on October 12th, 1969, when he boarded a DC 8 bound for Los

Angeles. This was the real beginning of his international career in the egg industry. Vagn's advice to him as he departed was "be honest - and when in doubt, use your gut feeling." Vagn remained as a valuable director on the Sanovo USA Board long after he stepped down as a board member of the parent company in Denmark. To this day he is Morten's sparring partner, advisor and a dear personal friend.

What role have associations played in shaping the industry? Morten admits he was never much of an association person. Because of his traveling it was difficult to be actively engaged in associations. One association though has meant a lot to him–the International Egg Commission. Its scope is international, with meetings in the different member countries throughout the world, and the people engaged in the IEC are from so many different countries. The uniqueness of the IEC is the fact that although competitors, IEC members at the annual gatherings seem to unite in a spirit of family togetherness. One reason may stem from the wise decision early on that the annual meeting is both business and social, where wives and husbands equally enjoy themselves in a relaxed atmosphere somewhere in the world. An egg processor in Chile may feel more at ease to discuss a problem with a fellow processor from, say Norway, than he would with his competitor down the road. Apart from the IEC, Morten said he was always fascinated with the outstanding job of Al Pope and his crew at the UEP. Al often would invite Morten to participate in the annual breakfast meetings held in conjunction with the international poultry exposition in Atlanta, Georgia. Morten truly enjoyed these meetings, the efficiency with which they were handled, and the professional manner in which issues were dealt with. The American way of running an association to Morten is fascinating. It is not a coincidence that the IEC turned a sharp corner when the dynamism of Al Pope swept through the organization while he was serving as chairman.

When asked what he would recommend to the upcoming generation, Morten said, "Think global – act local."

Torben Ernst 1918-2002

He knew egg products and he knew exporting. That gave him an edge. With his office at Odense, Denmark just meters away from the port, Torben Ernst would meet many ships' captains, along with the foreign seamen, loading and unloading their vessels. This location gave Torben another edge and a unique understanding as to what was needed to clear cargoes. After years of this education, he landed a job in a shipping company in northern Denmark. He spent a year with another shipping company in the Baltic city of Lubeck in Germany, where he perfected his German language, which would stay with him throughout his life. The war interrupted his international career, and he returned to Odense in 1939 where he got a job at the oldest registered company in Denmark, the flour mill Munke Molle. It was owned by a private family and the company dated back more than 900 years. In 1942 he left Munke Molle on the invitation of his boss Tage Klint, (1884-1953) who founded Lactosan, which would later grow into Lactosan-Sanovo Holding. Mr. Klint was out of an artistic family which was famous for Danish design and architecture, and he himself was full of ideas. One such idea was to make milk powders and dried egg powders, mix powders such as pancake mix, etc.

Torben started in the business way before there were any strict regulations in regards to egg processing, but as he was very conscious about quality, he initiated pasteurization at Lactosan long before this was common practice in Europe and the U.S.

In 1948 the company moved to new and larger facilities in Odense, but there were problems with getting egg supplies. The Danish egg production was on the rise, but the agricultural ministry would not permit large quotas for egg powder processing, as they were afraid that this would reduce the possibility to export fresh eggs, which was important for the country. However this was abandoned in 1950 and the company was free to operate as originally envisioned. At that time most of the production took place during the summer months when eggs were cheap and in supply, while sales were busiest during the winter when egg supply was short and prices higher.

As exportation of the finished egg powders started to take off,

Lactosan began to play with pasteurization. Salmonella at that time was already an issue and Torben saw the benefit of being able to supply Denmark, as well as the international market, with "safe" egg products.

One of the biggest changes he experienced in the industry therefore was the move from raw processed egg products to pasteurized products, but another idea which materialized in the early 70s was the commercialization of lyzosyme extraction from egg whites. Lactosan/Sanovo became the first egg products company to do so commercially through cooperation with the Italian pharmaceutical company SPA. The inauguration of this factory was in 1974. On another front, it was his foresight that led to Sanovo's expansion into the EU by the establishment of Sanovo Eiprodukte in Germany, which gave the Danish company its foothold inside the EU. Denmark did not become a member until nine years later.

Torben's oldest son Morten joined Lactosan/Sanovo in 1967 when Torben was in his late forties. Morten and Torben worked together until he passed away at 84 in 2002. He was also happy to work together with two grandchildren, Pernille, who was his secretary for 8 years, and Christoffer, who later became chief representative of Sanovo Engineering in China.

Torben would most certainly do it all over again, says his son, Morten. He started in the egg products industry as a young man and grew with it to become one of the most respected in the industry. He was one of the first to see the necessity of processing in different countries and lived to see his vision materialize.

As to people who meant the most to Torben, he would always remember his mentor, Tage Klint, who founded Lactosan and selected him as his right hand and successor. Later, Torben's close friend, Vagn Holck Andersen, was instrumental in bringing his vision to reality. Together they were a unique team. The older, conservative Torben and the younger, more aggressive Vagn made a perfect combination. Torben was a person who placed dignity and trust above all else in business, so some of his business relationships became close friends. It was more often than not that visitors who paid Sanovo in Odense a visit would find themselves at the Ernst dinner table at home enjoying whatever was on the menu for that day, rather than in a fancy restaurant. This was his style.

There are many stories about Torben Ernst, as he was a person with a great sense of humor and never shy of turning a dinner into a party. There is one story about Sander de Fluiter's first visit to Denmark. Sander de Fluiter of Nive fame in the Netherlands continued a close personal friendship until the end. Although competitors, he and Torben decided to meet in Copenhagen many years ago. This was their first such meeting and after a very successful dinner, Torben, being the host, insisted on walking Sander de Fluiter back safely to his hotel. Upon arriving at the hotel, Sander invited Torben in for a nightcap, which Torben later insisted to reciprocate at his own hotel nearby, and - so the story goes – this continued into the wee hours, walking each other back and forth between their respective hotels, having a nightcap each time. A lifelong friendship was established.

What would Torben have recommended for the new generation of egg people? He would surely advise honesty, a word is a word, and do your best.

CLIVE FRAMPTON

Framptons Limited, Somerset, England

Imagine your early childhood with memories of cracking eggs for "egg flip", a frozen egg product sold to bakeries. Whenever Clive Frampton, from Somerset, England, walks into a bakery today and enjoys the aroma of the pastries and pies, thoughts of his childhood, working for his Grandfather George's egg business and cracking eggs for an egg flip float through his mind.

"Eggs" are in the genes of the Frampton family, says Clive. Grandfather George started in the egg business over 100 years ago, in 1898, buying and selling eggs. Two world wars did not stop the Frampton egg business. George developed a successful egg packing business. George was a determined innovator and passed away as he would have wished; working at his desk at the age of 72. The business was then taken on by Clive's father, Norman.

In the early 1960s the business shifted from eggs into egg products. Today, the business is focused on the production of liquid food products, with a primary focus on value-added egg products.

Clive earned his degree in business finance. He became a director at the age of 21 years. In 1985 Clive was awarded a Nuffield Farming Scholarship which enabled him to visit the U.S. to study the egg products industry. This was a life-enhancing trip, which gave him many ideas for his business. Clive vividly recalls meeting Arthur Papetti and seeing the sheer scale of Papetti's Hygrade Eggs in Elizabeth, New Jersey, U.S. His trips to the States gave him a clear view of the potential development for the industry back home in the UK. In 1986 the UK was breaking less than 5% of our production. UK consumers today purchase about 23% of UK production as processed egg.

Clive's mentor in business was his father, Norman. Clive describes him as a wonderful man, full of energy, courage and ideas. He set Clive's path into egg processing and never retired from the business world. Over the last 30 years there have been huge changes in UK egg industry. Consolidation has perhaps been the most important. The UK has fewer companies, but stronger competitors. The customers are also fewer and larger. The strength of the retailers dominates the business agenda and profit margins are continually under pressure. This has caused structural changes in the industry with more processing plants being owned by egg-laying companies. The companies without their own egg-laying chickens are focusing on value-added products to protect their margins.

Over the years Clive has been involved with national, European and global egg associations. He recently served as Chairman of the International Egg Commission and was responsible for hiring the current Secretary General, Julian Madeley. Clive finds the industry associations of great benefit to the egg industry generally and also to his business. Sharing experiences with others from around the world helps Clive plan the forward momentum of Frampton's. Clive is supportive of working together with others in the egg business to protect and promote the interests of the industry. His business is now co-managed with his cousin, Ian Harvey.

As to the future? Clive says egg processors will become more Pan-European as the customers buy on a Pan-European basis. Margin pressures will encourage egg processors to move production to the south and east of Europe. Framptons will continue to focus on valued-added egg products and any other future challenges for this industry. Clive feels it's only natural. After all, eggs are in his genes!

JURGEN FUCHS GMBH & CO.

Altenhoeferweg 29 Germany

The pressure was a great load on his chest. Jurgen Fuchs was flush with eggs and desperately needed a place to sell them. His usual customers in Germany didn't need the eggs. Other markets still needed time to develop. So, Jurgen placed a call to his friend, Arthur Papetti, of Papetti's Hygrade Eggs, Elizabeth, New Jersey USA. Arthur had purchased a few container loads from Jurgen in the past. Perhaps he could help out this time. Jurgen described the calls with Arthur in this fashion: First they talked about price. Once that was agreed upon, they discussed quantity. This time, after reaching the price, Arthur asked, "How many containers?" Jurgen said unhesitatingly, "One hundred." There was a moment of silence on the other end of the line, but then Arthur squeezed out an "okay." Jurgen's heart soared high as the pressure he was feeling was instantly released. The relationship between the two continued to grow, and to this day, Jurgen says that Arthur Papetti would have to be among the greatest in influencing his life in the egg business. Arthur is one who can make decisions in a matter of seconds on large orders.

Jurgen started in the egg business in 1965, taking over for his father. Jurgen credits his father with helping him to meet many important people in the egg business. These relationships continued throughout his career, and today, Jurgen knows and conducts business deals with people throughout the world. At meetings of the International Egg Commission, Jurgen can be seen discussing some opportunity with his egg processing friends and other marketers from around the world.

Jurgen noted that the biggest change for his business was the founding of the European Union. That's when Germany changed from being an importing country to one that exports. Suppliers in other countries were not able to export to the EU anymore. Jurgen searched for and found new markets in the Far East and Middle East. Changes in the EU continued with consumers opting more and more for eggs from alternative production systems. Now, with a ban on cages looming in the near future, Jurgen was quick to point out that the ban on cages in Germany should not be unilateral, but consistent with all of Europe when changes are made in egg production. Looking back, Jurgen admits openly that the one thing he would do differently, if he could change what he's done, is not to get involved in egg production. Jurgen sees the future as one involving more consumption of egg products and less of shell eggs. No doubt, Jurgen will continue to position his business opportunities to align with what the consumer wants. He is pleased to have enjoyed a life in the egg business, calling it dynamic, fascinating and full of opportunities.

Dan Gardner

When he interviewed for his first job, the recruiter asked Dan Gardner how much money he wanted to make. He responded, "You'll never pay me enough." And that is how Dan saw his worth, always reaching higher and higher. After 41 years in the egg business and becoming the CEO of the MG Waldbaum Company, Wakefield, Nebraska, Dan helped the company became one of the largest egg products companies in the U.S. with gross sales exceeding $200 million and more than 1,200 employees. Dan sold the business in 1990 and started the Gardner Foundation with $12 million, which contributes hundreds of thousands of dollars annually to institutions, groups and organizations. The Foundation continues to grow and make contributions annually. Even after selling MG Waldbaum to Michael Foods, Inc., Dan continued striving to reach his goal through his Foundation right up to his death on January 19, 2001. One of Dan's favorite institutions was Wayne State College, which named the Gardner Building in Dan's honor. Dan served as a trustee of the Wayne State Foundation, and established the Daniel W. Gardner Endowment of Athletic Scholarships to Wayne State College in 1991.

From early in his career, Dan Gardner wanted to run his own business. At 26 years of age, he traveled from the Bronx in New York City to Wakefield, Nebraska in March 1952 at the invitation of Milton G. Waldbaum. When asked if Dan wanted to partner with Milt, he said, he didn't think Wakefield was big enough for the both of them. Milton Waldbaum settled that concern by going off to medical school in Omaha. But on Thursdays the two partners would get together to have dinner and discuss the business.

With fewer than 50 employees, MG Waldbaum Company started. The egg breaking was done by hand. After women candled the eggs by hand, the good quality eggs would be placed on one belt while the poor quality in baskets on another belt. The women were very proficient and could break as many as 2.5 cases per hour. If they were breaking whole egg, they could break as many as 5 cases an hour (600 cases per hour for an 8 hour shift or 4800 cases. The same women who candled eggs would also break the eggs out of the baskets at night. At one time, MG Waldbaum Company had 120 women breaking eggs. Gross sales were less than $1 million.

In 1978 MG Waldbaum Company purchased their own chickens, since many of the local farmers were moving from chickens to larger farm animals. At first, the money to build the chicken house and put in 60,000 birds came from Milt's doctor friends. Later the financing came from three individuals that Dan remembered with appreciation: Dr. Halsey (President of Wayne State College), Dr. Swanson and Dave Kruse, a computer operator. Dan made sure the company had sales for the eggs before they put the chickens in (he called that a reverse operation - different from the others). In the trucking side of the business the drivers would pick up eggs from the farms with some stops collecting as few as 2-3 cases. The drivers also gave green stamps with the eggs. One stamp for each dozen eggs was the premium.

With the automation of the processing plant, Dan worked on the machines themselves. They were air operated. They would practice with hard boiled eggs, but when they switched over to the fresh eggs, the eggs went every direction. Dan heard about a company in Denmark that was making egg breaking machines. He traveled there, liked what he saw and bought six machines. At a show in Europe, he also saw a machine that colored eggs for the Easter market. He bought that too. Dan had been quoted as saying the success of the business was the good people working there. It was also moving forward with the newest technology in processing equipment.

MG Waldbaum Company was one of the pioneers in pasteurization. Their contract with Campbell's Soup Company prompted MG Waldbaum Company to find ways to deliver a product to meet their customer's specification, meaning no salmonella or other bacteria. They experimented with heat pasteurization, picking up a trick or two from those who pasteurized milk. It worked! The product produced had plate counts less than 3,000 and were salmonella-negative. Approximately three years later, the federal government pressed the industry to pasteurize. The industry fought the effort, saying that it would ruin the egg quality, and the product wouldn't perform. Dan kept quiet since MG Waldbaum Company was already producing pasteurized product and had been doing so for years. When the law passed, MG Waldbaum Company had a head start over others in the industry.

Dan was actively involved in dealings in Washington, DC, and that proved useful to his business. He described one time how he had problems with a particular lot of product not meeting government specifications. He flew to Washington and sat down with Senator Curtiss, who chaired the Senate Armed Forces Committee. Dan explained the problems with the product, noting that it was perfectly good egg product. It just didn't meet certain specifications. The Senator telephoned a particular General in the U.S. Army to came over to meet them. After explaining the product differences to the General, the Senator asked Dan to go for a walk and come back in a few hours. When he returned, he had a customer for the product.

Part of Dan's legacy also will be the continuing egg work of industry, government, and association egg people that he mentored over the years. Dean Hughson remembers that Dan was an amazing teacher of business. "How many young employees get an opportunity to make million dollar decisions? Dan did that to many of us who worked for him and even when we were wrong only asked us if we learned from it? He was an amazing man and is missed today in the industry."

In the egg industry, Dan served as director of Egg Clearinghouse, Inc.; director of the Poultry and Egg Institute of America; director of the Nebraska Poultry Industries; director of Midwest Egg Producers; director of United Egg Producers; and Chairman of the International Trade Committee to the International Egg Commission. Dan is survived by his wife, Jeanne; two sons, David and Kirk; a daughter and her husband, Leslie and Tim Beebe; and nine grandchildren–Adam, Brooke, Jordan, Ross, Kyle, Carly Gardner, Javannah, Timarie and Garek Bebee.

ELLIOT GIBBER

Deb-El Foods

Elizabeth, NJ

Every successful business starts with a business plan. His successful business began with a dream and a sheer determination to make it work. Elliot Gibber's background is a testament to his determination and how he has made his egg breaking business a success.

Coming from Russia, his grandfather started off in Detroit, then moved East. The family was in the hotel business at first, but due in large part to a deep religious conviction against operating on Saturday, they entered the poultry business. This included contract chicken production in approximately 15 locations, a hatchery, and a feed mill.

In the 1960s, the family built a modern layer complex and processing facility based in Thompsonville, New York. In the 1970s, the family was marketing liquid eggs and shell eggs in New York City until a major fire forced the shell egg production side of the business to close. The breaking side continued. Elliot later went to work for Julius Tauber and ran his breaking operation in Florida, but later came north to New Jersey. In the 1980s he had the dream of building an egg drying plant, and his dream became a reality with the opening of his Deb-El Foods drying plant in 1984. During the planning stages Elliot developed close contacts with numerous overseas customers.

Elliot continued with his dreams of building his business. In the 1990s he bought Ballas Food Products, a distributor of a full line of liquid, frozen and dried egg products, then located in the Bronx area of New York City.

Shortly thereafter, Elliot purchased a mayonnaise and co-packing company located in Bayonne, NJ, and he began selling a full line of mayonnaise, salad dressings, powdered drink mixes and other co-packed products. He later moved the Ballas egg product distribution business to the Bayonne facility.

In early 2000 Elliot took another step forward when he bought his father's breaking operation and expanded and remodeled it in the ensuing years to the point where it is now a new breaking operation, processing and packing a full line of liquid and frozen egg products from 5 lb. containers right up to tankers.

Elliot took over the chairmanship of United Egg Association in 2001, and kept that position for two years. His leadership helped place the association on sound financial footing. Elliot's sheer determination in forming his business spilled over into his chairmanship. He was committed to strengthening UEA, or closing its doors altogether. He succeeded, and UEA is sound today.

Elliot has a large family. His son, Daniel Gibber, is Vice President of Sales. Jacob is in Israel serving as a rabbinical teacher. Marc is a third year medical student at the Albert Einstein School of Medicine. Michael is a student graduating from Yeshiva University and will enter the egg/real estate business shortly. Mindy is a sophomore at Yeshiva University's Stern College for Women, and David is in his first year at Yeshiva University High School. Elliot and his wife, Debbie, have six grandchildren.

Elliott is active in many organizations. He is the Chairman of the Board of Manhattan Day School, is a National Sr. VP of the Union of Orthodox Congregations of America (OU), is a member of the R.I.E.T.S.

Board of Yeshiva University, and serves as the Technical Advisor to American Egg Board on further processed products.

Elliot has focused his career on breaking and drying eggs. He has seen the industry change to the point where one must be vertically integrated, from chickens to the end-user. He says the "Big guys got bigger leaving a niche market for smaller guys." What's going to happen in the future? Twenty years from now, Elliot sees that the people who have expanded their businesses into mega companies will divest themselves, and start splitting apart.

The biggest obstacle facing the industry, Elliot feels, is the lack of cooperation between the shell egg and egg product sides of the industry.

Elliot credits much of his success to what he learned from his father, as well as to his successful association with Arthur Papetti. "I am where I am today because of Arthur Papetti being a good friend," said Elliot. "If the industry doesn't learn from the Arthur Papettis of the world, the industry is doomed," he added.

What are Elliot's plans for the future? He wants to work until he can transmit his knowledge and "know-how" to the next generation. That sounds like Elliot. His sheer determination will no doubt be the vehicle for accomplishing his goal.

JOAQUIN GOMEZ GOMEZ (1932-1994)

In 1969 Mr. Joaquin Gomez Gomez pioneered the liquid egg industry in Mexico when he created Alimentos de la Granja in Mexico City.

He began in the feed industry and while working with the Romero family in Tehuacan, where he saw the potential for buying eggs broken by hand at the farms, processing them and then selling the liquid egg products to companies like Bimbo, Continental Baking and Kraft.

In the early years he developed contacts with a young Morten Ernst and Dick Smith, who helped him set up the first automatic egg breaking machines (Sanovo 500s), filtration, cooling, pasteurization and packaging systems. At this time he was also able to provide standardized egg products to his customers when he purchased a refractometer from a young Mike Harris at the University of California. He traveled around the U.S. to learn new techniques and processing ideas, developing friendships along the way with people like Don Paulsen.

Being the first egg breaking plant in Mexico, he had to work hand in hand with the Mexican government to write regulations to govern the egg products industry. Those regulations remained in effect until the mid 90s.

Through the years he was the sole supplier in Mexico of pasteurized liquid and frozen egg products and helped Bimbo set up their first egg breaking plant in Atzcapotzalco.

Today, his wife Mercedes, one daughter and four sons survive Joaquin. Alimentos de la Granja continues to operate producing a wide array of liquid, frozen and dried egg products, while one of his sons went on to work for Diamond Systems as the manager for all egg breaker and further processing projects thoughout the world.

BRAD HALPERN, EGGOLOGY

California is not just Hollywood. Egg Whites Hatch in LA.

A self-described "oddity" for getting into the egg business, Brad Halpern formed his own company, Eggology, back in 1993. A Los

Angeles native, he grew increasingly active in the sport of Triathlon after his graduation from USC, earning a BA degree in marketing. Brad enjoyed the physical challenge and the intense training involved in preparing for 20-25 grueling races per season, while working as an advertising executive for Arbitron Ratings and other ad firms.

After spending hours separating eggs to get the whites, Brad packaged fresh liquid egg whites in easy-to-handle clear plastic jars, the beginning of Eggology. Like many athletes, he was routinely consuming 6-8 egg whites for breakfast each day as a way to maintain protein intake while avoiding the fat and cholesterol found in whole eggs. He was still working at an advertising firm when he asked his wife Robyn to try to sell Eggology to gyms and health clubs where body builders and personal trainers already knew the benefits of egg whites, and would welcome the convenience of the packaged product. Art Berman, one of the owners of Hi Point Industries, gave Brad a 10' x 10' space in a loft at his factory to start marketing his product. Thirty days later Brad quit his job and became an oddity to the egg industry. It wasn't long before chefs, dietitians, bakers and the Hollywood elite discovered the benefits of fresh, pure egg whites, with no additives or preservatives. Since entering into the egg industry in 1993, Brad experienced the power of the USDA. The trend toward manufacturers offering egg product line-extensions in a non-expanding dairy case had resulted in "brick and mortar retailers" becoming empowered to squeeze manufacturers and distributors into padding their lines by demanding free-fills, mediocre advertising, and other hidden slotting fees. On the brighter side, as the food conglomerates consolidated and have taken over most of the chain store shelves, the public's support of specialty retailers offers a refreshing reprieve from the trend. Would Brad do it over again? Despite all the "blood, sweat, and tears" of diving into the egg industry – it has been a great and learning journey, he said. "Although, Brad added, "In my next life, I will hopefully choose a food product that is neither perishable, or federally regulated."

What was Brad's most memorable experience? Having spent $150,000 to construct a new egg plant, and having been assisted by the USDA circuit supervisor, and conferring with USDA tech support in Omaha, NE, Brad prepared for the meeting with USDA. Brad memorized the entire USDA regulation handbook all the way down to the slip coefficient of the production floor. The day came to receive the "Grant of Inspection." The circuit supervisor inspected the new state-of-the-art plant. There were four individuals from the Omaha Tech. Center on the phone, all of whom were baffled by the possibility of opening a new plant, because a new egg plant hadn't opened in 24 years, and no one was willing to be accountable to give the green light, Brad theorized. Brad mentioned that he did hear lots of "hems and haws" while they shuffled papers and whispered. Finally, the circuit supervisor said, "I see no reason why this plant should not be allowed to immediately begin production." One of the tech people said, "But, we don't have the plant blueprints." Brad had been told by the tech support that blueprints were not necessary and he repeated that into the phone. The circuit supervisor then asked, "Are blueprints required?" They responded, "Well, they are no longer required, but we do like to see them." At that moment I should have thrown my key to the plant into the trash and gone into selling copiers," said Brad. Nonetheless, the circuit supervisor pushed and Brad got the "grant" that day.

Who had a great impact on Brad's career? Milton, who was the dairy manager at a Wild Oats Market that was back in a day when dairy managers could make decisions, lamented Brad. Eggology was only being sold in gyms at the time when he walked into Milton's store and sold him the half gallon clear bottle of egg whites. He took two cases that day, and three more cases the following week. He soon referred Brad to two other dairy managers at other Wild Oats stores, who did the same. Eleven months later Brad received a call from The Wild Oats

Corporate office saying he was not an approved vendor, despite the fact that the product was successfully being sold at all their 63 stores at the time.

Brad deserves to have his name right along the Hollywood stars at Gruman's Chinese Theater Walk of Stars.

Mr. Wei Han,

Chairman of Dalian Hanwei Enterprise Group,

China

Dalian Hanwei Enterprise Group, named after the chairman, Mr. Wei Han, is the biggest egg producer of China, and also the biggest abalone breeder in the world. The company started 23 years ago with 50 chickens and now has 3 million layers.

In 1982, soon after China permitted private business, Mr. Wei Han started his business. Only 10 years later, Dalian Hanwei Group was established, which was also the first private enterprise group established in China. Now the group has 13 companies involved in the business of layer rising, egg processing, sea-farming, health supplement development and production.

Many people in China thought what Mr. Han had achieved was a miracle, considering the nature of the business. To anyone who knows Mr. Han personally, he is a down-to-earth businessman, a faithful Buddhist, a caring husband and a loving father.

Mr. Han was born in the Dongnihe Village, suburb of the City Dalian, a coastal city northeast of China. He was born the ninth child, with five sisters and three brothers. The family lived in poverty, just like most others at the time. Han was a quiet and smart boy and, unlike other kids, he had a lot of interest in learning. However at that time, in a family with so many children, not everyone had the luxury to learn in school. At the age of 15, Han had to quit school to start working.

The first time he went to the city on the back of the carriage, he was so excited by all the things he had never seen before in the village. Today, he still remembers vividly what he saw and thought. "There were so many vehicles in the city and it looked busy and exciting. There were great tall buildings I'd never seen before, even though today they are just apartment blocks you can find everywhere in a Chinese city. The city people looked at us and I saw disgust in their eyes. That was when I thought to myself, I would not live like this forever. I will own one of those great buildings." When Mr. Han said this, he appeared calm behind his large, dark oak table. He now owns one 15-story office complex in the heart of the city. He had achieved much more than the ambition of that 15 year old boy.

With such ambition, Han started to take advantage of all the opportunities to learn new skills. He was the old carpenters' favorite apprenticeship, and the farmers' favorite helper. Soon enough, he was appreciated for the work he was doing and his opinions were respected. In a few years, he got a job in the town council working as the assistant of the agricultural minister, one of the youngest officials.

During those years, a job in the government was considered a job that would provide you with the "golden bowl," meaning that you can depend on it to provide comfort and wealth for the rest of your life.

With such a job to envy, Han started to search for the other half of his life, a supporting wife. Mrs. Han is now the general manager of Dalian Pacific Seafood Company under Dalian Hanwei Group. She is a sharp and interesting woman with a lot of ideas. Her Hailongxian health supplement extracted from abalone, sea cucumber and sea urchin made a great success on the market since it was launched in 2001. She has been with the group in every step of its development and took up many roles wherever she was needed.

Twenty-four years ago, Mr. Han was an energetic young guy with a great job; Mrs. Han was this smart girl, famous in the town for her beauty. They first met one cold winter night, arranged by each other's parents. They exchanged a passport size photo of each other and a few sentences. Until today, Mr. Han still keeps the photo in his wallet. He said, "I didn't know someone perfect for me existed, until I saw her. I knew from the beginning that we will be together for the rest of my life, and the next lives." On that little black and white photo, Mrs. Han looked young and pretty, her hair in braids at one side. Only the trendy girls back then tied their hair this way. They got married shortly after they met, but soon realized they had got into a financial crisis having spent too much on their dream wedding. With their first child arriving, they found themselves struggling with 37RMB wages from the government every month (approximately 4 dollars).

In Han's job as the assistant of the agriculture minister, he had the opportunity to gather first hand information on the changes of government policies and the supply and demand of agricultural products. He was one of the first to open to the idea of private business, and also one of the first to realize there is a huge gap between the supply and demand of eggs in the city. He ran through the idea of starting his own chicken farm again and again, but was not sure how to tell the family.

Mrs. Han supported his idea whole-heartedly, surprising almost everyone. Mr. Han was surer than ever that she understood him more than anyone else, and was determined to make this business a success.

With the birth of their first child, Han quit his job in the town council and set up Hanwei Chicken Farm with 50 chickens, in 1982.

The company borrowed 3000 RMB, which was a huge amount of money at the time, considering an official's wage per month was only 37 RMB. All the villagers gossiped about this extraordinary turn of events. They could not understand what this meant and predicted that Han would bring disaster to his family.

The market was like a sponge in those early days. Anything produced was immediately absorbed. The farm was instantly a success.

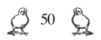

The other family members started to join in. Han's two elder brothers both got involved. The whole family worked closely with each other, raising the chickens and selling the eggs.

When the birds got ill and no one knew what to do about it, they were not able to employ any veterinarian due to the nature of the business. People were still worried to be part of a private company. Mrs. Han, the highest qualified member of the family, took up the thick book for poultry veterinarian, and learned about the diseases by operating on the sick chickens. She would lay the book on one side of the table and the sick chicken on the other side, and then read from page to page to work out what was wrong with the chicken.

Unlike other villagers who also started to build their own farms, who saved all the money they earned to try to pay back the debts, Han invested the profit back to expand the farm. Instead of just working in the farm and selling the eggs, Han spent a lot of time with his wife calculating. They were making sure the farm expanded at a healthy speed.

Only one year later, in 1983, Han expanded his farm to 800 layers, in three-farm houses, one of the largest in the city. The town council picked him to represent the other farms in a meeting in the city. Han understood the importance of this chance to talk to the city council. He grabbed the opportunity and made a memorable impression. He said on that day, he would expand the farm to over 10,000 layers. Almost everyone was surprised by this young man's ambition, and could not help but be influenced by his enthusiasm. Right after the meeting, the town council received instructions from the city to help the work of Mr. Han.

Today, having the largest layer farm in China already, Han is working on a 10 million-layer farm in Fuxin. The project will be complete with an egg processing plant. Many people looked at this project the same way people looked at Han when he was talking about that 10,000-layer farm 22 years ago. Han was only more determined that he would be able make it work.

In 1984, being the most successful young farmer from the Northeast, Han got the chance to go abroad, to Japan, with a group of young businessmen led by the government. The group also had a reception with the Japanese prime minister at that time.

Going abroad was something people only dream about in the village. Everything they saw in Japan was never seen before. Han knew very well his priority and did not hesitate to ask to see a Japanese chicken farm. That was one of the most memorable experiences for Han, and changed his idea of the poultry business. He realized that his idea of a 10,000-layer farm was very small indeed. There, he first saw chickens in cages, eggs collected on a conveyor belt, and operations fully automated.

One year after he came back from Japan, he was ready to build a farm just like the one he saw. He asked the bank for 150,000 RMB. This action of Han hit the news immediately. People were talking about how would this young farmer get so much nerve! Today, Chinese people use "Wan Yuan Hu" (Owner of 10,000 RMB) to address the wealthy people. 150,000 RMB sounded shocking to all.

By 1987 Han had 150,000 chickens. The same year, joint venture Weijia Chicken Farm Company was established as one of the first Joint Venture Companies in the City of Dalian. Now, Han has become one of the eight top businessmen in the City of Dalian, at 29.

Han, influenced by his mother, is a religious Buddhist. In 1988, when he was praised for his success, he thought more about the meaning of all this, and felt it was his responsibility to help others. In that year, with the support of his wife, he spent the profit of the whole year to build the village a new primary school, while also refusing to have the school named after him by the thankful villagers.

In 1991, just when the business was going from good to better, Han lost the most important person of his life, his mother. She was just like most other old Chinese ladies, peaceful and loving. Even during the most difficult days in the fifties, she never complained or cried. She did her part of the job and was grateful for any outcome. When her son became the most successful business man in the village, she cared more about whether he was caring enough for others.

When she passed away, Han moved the whole family from the city to the village to "Shouxiao" (shows respect to the deceased) for three years. He deeply regretted that the business took too much of his time and he never had enough time keep his mother company. The sadness did not stop him from taking the next significant step forward.

In 1992, on the 19th of August, one of the most important events in the history of modern Chinese market economy took place in the People's Parliament. The host of the event was Mr. Wei Han. The guests were party leaders and ministers. The event was the establishment of Dalian Hanwei Group, the first private enterprise group of the People's Republic of China.

The national news reported the event, describing it as the landmark event. More than 500 journalists from all over the world participated in the press conference. "This event showed that private business is finally approved officially." "Now, in the red White House of China, the Chinese government warmly received the first private enterprise group of China!" "It is indeed the landmark event of the development of the Chinese non-governmental companies!"

With the establishment of the Group, Han started to stretch to other areas, in order to divert the risk of poultry breeding. There was an old saying in China, that no matter how much money you have, you should not count on the animals you owned. Soon after the establishment of the group, Han invested in "HENGTONG" office complex, in the heart of the city, an advertising company, a soft drink company, an IT company, a trading company and Dalian Pacific Seafood Company.

That was the time when the demand for eggs was still growing steadily and the press was paying a lot of attention to the development of the Group. Somehow, Mrs. Han started to get worried about the rapid growth of the company.

When the market economy first started, the market was starving. A lot of businesses grew rapidly, and a lot of businessmen became big-headed. Thinking back to the earlier days, the others who got the same fame as Han in the city of Dalian had all failed when they had to deal with the more mature and reasonable market.

Han invested in so many new companies at the same time, especially the 130 million RMB investment in Dalian Pacific Seafood Company, it was not long before the Group experienced its first major cash flow problem.

In 1994, Han was forced to decide whether to continue with so many companies. After a heated discussion, new companies were closed and only Dalian Pacific Seafood Company was kept. It seemed to be a good idea to divert risk when they decided to invest in these companies, however the idea to divert risk actually brought to the Group much more risk. The Group chose to focus on what it is best at, raising laying hens.

Just when Han and his wife thought they closely avoided the downfall, they found themselves in worse shape than ever. The demand for eggs had stopped growing.

In all those years, the Hanwei Chicken Farm never had an egg storage warehouse. In 1995, for the first time, the market stopped absorbing all the products. The eggs started to fill up in the factory. The company got in the red after a year.

Han was not worried about the change. In fact, just the opposite . . . he was excited. In the 1996 annual meeting, he talked to the other members of the committee. With his charisma, he persuaded everyone that this was only temporary, most farms would not be able to get though with the market situation, but they would, being the largest and the most professional. In fact, not only that, they would be able to expand.

They decided to expand the farm from 500,000 layers to 2 million. Han believed that with more and more farms closing down, the market would soon pick up. This had always been the trend of the market. Similar strategy was successful on a smaller scale in the past. This time, Han was sure that when the market picked up with in a year, the Hanwei Chicken Farm would again be the first to benefit.

The market did not bounce back in a year.

All the chicken farmers in China were struggling, and not only the chicken farmers, but other agricultural businesses were also facing an almost saturated market. Rather than choosing another struggling area of business, most egg farmers chose to stay with what they were best at. The Hanwei Group, which always put the product quality first, would now differentiate their eggs from the others.

Han managed to persuade the bankers with his extraordinary enthusiasm and respectable work. The Group was going to become the first brand egg provider and the only company to export raw eggs to Japan.

In China, there is an old saying: Disasters come in pairs. In 1995, the Chinese government tightened the banks' investment. In 1997, the Asia economic crisis happened. During those times, the egg prices fell. On top of all these, from 1990 to 2000, the "red tide" occurred 49 times. Hundreds of millions of RMB worth of abalones bred by the Dalian Pacific Seafood Company all died in the sea.

Dalian Pacific Seafood Company was one of the three out of twenty abalone-breeders in Dalian who survived from this disaster. Mrs. Han took over the company at this most difficult time.

With Mrs. Han working on the Pacific Seafood Company, Han's focus turned back to eggs. He went forward with his idea of Green Eggs. The first branded eggs, "GEGEDA" eggs were born in 1999. "GEGEDA" is now the "country's famous brand," certified by the official board. It was the only agricultural product with such a certificate.

Han, member of the Chinese Congress for the past seven years, took advantage of press opportunities to promote his idea of Green Eggs. In China, Green products, similar to the organic products aboard, became popular in major cities. That was when Han set up the Beijing and Shanghai Green Food Company, to market and sell "GEGEDA" eggs to these two major cities and surrounding areas.

Eggs in China were only sold loose before GEGEDA came to the market. The name itself was easy to remember, as it was the sound of hens when laying eggs. People were not only attracted by the idea of healthier eggs, but also by the friendly design.

GEGEDA became the star of the agricultural product market. It has inspired many in the business.

At the same time, Mrs. Han was not beaten by the natural disaster. She relied on technology to bring the Pacific Seafood back on its feet. By allowing the Science Institution to experiment on abalone for free at the Pacific Company, the company became the only one in China to successfully breed triploid abalone. The company is now the largest abalone seeds breeder of the world. Later, together with the China Science Institution, the company developed a health supplement, which made an instant success on the market. The Group now was closer to its

consumers than ever.

Many people searched for the common personality of successful business persons. Was it ambition, enthusiasm, innovation, or vision? At the end of the search, they would probably find out that they all had very different personalities. Indeed, there was something they share–that is stamina and strong willpower. That was how they were the ones to get through the most difficult times.

In 2000, Hanwei Group became the country member of the International Egg Commission. In 2002, Han appeared in Forbes as the 43rd most wealthy man in China. In 2003, Hanwei Group drafted the Egg Products Standard for the official board of China.

Sitting in his office overlooking the 3-million-layer farm, Han looked beyond what he had achieved. "Now is the time to take our products abroad."

The Hanovo Foods Company, established in 2004, would be able to produce 5000 tons of egg powder every year. This remarkable company combined with the largest and most experienced layer-farm of China, attracted the attention of everyone in related businesses. In the same way that GEGEDA changed the consumer's idea of egg shopping, Hanovo would also lead the changes of the egg products market.

Han's ambitious 10 million layers farm in FUXIN would be his next leap forward. The new industrial farming would bring to the consumers safer and healthier eggs. Han said, "The back yard chicken farming will become history sooner or later, the sooner the better for everyone." Many problems were raised due to the back yard chicken farming in the Chinese countryside. Those farms were neither hygienic nor isolated, thus diseases spread between farms easily and frequently. There is no doubt that soon Han will be taking the egg industry of China to the next level of development.

Mike Harris in His Own Words

For me, it all started in 1965 with a new egg breaking plant at Safeway Stores, in Riverside, CA. I was attending the University of California, Riverside, studying microbiology. The manager of the new plant, Richard L. Miller, called my professor and asked if there was a student who could set up and operate a laboratory on a part time basis. I got the job and started in 1967, having thought little about eggs, much less mechanically breaking and pasteurizing them. I worked for Safeway and later as a USDA Egg Products Inspector for about 3 years. In 1968, I received my BS degree and got introduced to egg drying at the old Southwestern Egg Producers plant in Riverside.

As years went by, I worked at a number of companies like Nulaid Foods, National Foods Corp, and Deb-El Foods as plant manager, and gained a lot of experience in egg products as well as learning some of the engineering that goes into building new plants. Along the way, I met my wife Susi in an egg plant. She has been patient with me through so many years of long hours and time away from home.

In 1990, I went to work at Seymour Foods, to help build and start up new plants, such as ISE Farms, Crystal Lake Farms and ASA Puerto Rico, as well as new plants in Mexico, Colombia, South Africa and Europe. In 1996, I joined Diamond Systems working with the new inline breaking machines, as well as building new processing plants, finishing with a large, new plant in China.

In 2000, I retired from all the traveling and excitement. But, during my 25+ years, I had the opportunity to be involved with the E 3A Sanitary Standards Committee, served as technical liaison with the Food and Dairy 3A Steering Committee, and as Chairman of the newly formed UEA Egg Products Technical Committee, as we launched the Egg Pasteurization studies.

The most satisfying change I have seen in the industry, other than new plants and machines come into production, is to have seen the egg breaking industry transform from a "salvage" industry to a full-fledged member of the food industry, and to see egg products accepted for their outstanding nutritional and functional properties. It has been a great opportunity to be part of the changes in breaking and processing equipment and processes. What a time it has been . . . and will continue to be I am sure!

I have been truly lucky to have worked with a number of great people in the industry–people like Rodney Voorhees (USDA), Rich Miller (my mentor), Dick Smith (FES), Torben Ernst (Lactosan), O.R. "Andy" Anderson (Seymour), Sidney Weil (Nulaid), Jim Nield (Diamond) and the Danish "Prince"–Morten Ernst. These people, and so many others, like the Dr. Hans Lineweaver and his group at Western Regional Laboratory, have truly made the industry exciting and so very memorable. So many have worked their entire lives in this business, and their efforts are what have made this industry grow–and we have had the best that nature can offer as a raw material.

I think that the United Egg Association has had a tremendous impact to the benefit of the industry. The formation of the Technical Committee and the egg pasteurization studies are just the beginning. The industry will continue to become more and more technical, and a strong organization to coordinate all the developments between the regulatory and technical aspects and to continue to satisfy our customers is essential. I think a strong organization that is willing to pool its resources is essential to our continued growth as an industry.

I would expect that all the many components of the egg that give it such a broad range of uses will eventually be fractionated and modified, in ways unknown now, to give our customers and consumers an ever more diversified nutritional and functional natural product. And I think those who will drive these developments will have the vision and technical expertise to explore and develop THE EGG.

A wish for the future would be to see the industry be able to work with the regulators more closely as partners rather than as adversaries– "like we did in the old days"–our goals are still the same–to provide wholesome and safe egg products to the consumer.

Kit Henningsen

When most people say of their career they would gladly do what they did all over again, he said he would rather have run a surf shop in Barbados or sold Ferraris in Hong Kong. It is no reflection on his success in sales, but it does reflect his frankness in speaking his mind. Kit Henningsen, a fourth-generation eggman, was enormously successful in selling egg products. In addition to travels all over the USA, Kit has made sales trips and calls for Henningsen Foods in thirty foreign countries. He grew up in Pelham Manor, NY and went away to school at the age of 14. After graduating from the Lawrenceville School and The University of Virginia, he started as a Regional Sales Manager (Domestic Market), eventually gained responsibility for Latin America, then National Sales (Domestic), and now 29 years later, serves as the VP of International Sales. When asked to participate in this book on industry leaders, Kit said the "gas for the engine" in this industry are the plant and production managers. They are the ones who should be interviewed. He also praised the plant people he works with, saying their rock solid support and dedication to product quality helped make his job successful.

In analyzing the industry today, Kit says fewer hands and less product knowledge run the industry on the buying side. Today's typical egg products buyer lacks the technical product knowledge and market experience buyers had 20 years ago. Kit acknowledges, "This is not the buyer's fault — it is the result of having responsibility for too many different products to become really knowledgeable about any of them." He added, "Many sellers are now equally guilty — they sell price, not product."

As to the future of the egg industry, Kit feels it depends on the players' ability to master simple math. Too many chickens mean disastrous losses — fewer chickens mean healthy profits. The industry can't (won't) find the balance.

While U.S. consolidations may happen, Kit foresees foreign eggs and egg products eventually entering (and complicating) the domestic products market. Speaking from hard-learned lessons, Kit says that the domestic players have no idea how sophisticated the foreign producers are. Competition from Latin America, China, India, and, of course, Europe, will eventually be on the U.S. doorstep and "making plenty of noise."

Kit sees the advancements being made with technology, but it will be driven by marketability and price.  Buyers will continue to buy the cheapest possible product which will work in their particular application — so the emphasis will be on reduced costs rather than improved products. Issues will play a large role in the future such as Environmental / Animal Rights issues (Green Party / Greenpeace / PETA). These will drive production costs higher.

In spite of this, Kit says that products will improve with an emphasis on high performance albumen (gel strength / high whip) and lower incidence of salmonella, listeria, etc, through breakthroughs in hygienic handling and other breakthroughs. Eventually (far away and after bad episodes) Kit hopes that Avian Influenza will become a more manageable issue, either through improved avian / veterinary medicine or more tightly managed / segregated flocks.

People who have impacted Kit's life include Dr. Dwight Berquist, a brilliant man whose contributions to the technical side of the dehydrated egg business and to Henningsen Foods in particular cannot be measured. In addition to his formidable genius, Kit says Dwight was a good and decent man who had the respect and friendship of all who knew him. He was a quiet industry giant. He also added Food Brokers Jim Dawson in Chicago and Tom Churchill in Boston, who took the time to teach Kit how the industrial side of the U.S. food business works. They were his mentors and he says he will forever respect their integrity, business acumen, patience, and willingness to help when Kit was starting out. They were two exceptional gentlemen (and were themselves friends) who left a very strong, positive impression on Kit.

When it comes to the contributions by trade associations - - Jim Sumner and his staff at USAPEEC get an A+ from Kit. Sumner's group are aggressive and effective promoters of U.S. egg products worldwide. Kit manages many foreign brokers and distributors around the world - they all know USAPEEC and have nothing but high praise for their promotional activities.

What would Kit recommend for the incoming generation of people in the egg industry? A sense of humor and a thick skin. He added, keep a travel bag packed and a current passport, as this is now a worldwide (not exclusively USA) market. Also, be computer literate and communication portable - know your product line - speak Spanish and Chinese. Hit the lotto. Have a back-up career (law or medical degree very useful), marry rich, and strongly encourage every kid in your neighborhood to throw dozens of eggs on Mischief Night and Halloween. (We told you already about his frankness).

Kit reflects on all his travels and says "These are the experiences I value most as this exposure to places and cultures has given me many good friends and has made me further appreciate what a blessing it is to be an American selling American products."

Vic Henningsen

Few companies can boast of being in the egg business for more than 100 years, but the Henningsen Companies, founded in 1889, is proud of their four generations in this industry. The company handled all forms of poultry, eggs, dairy products including ice cream - all produced in the Shanghai plant. Vic Henningsen II was the last President and CEO before the company was sold to the QP Corporation in 1990. Vic became Chairman Emeritus, and continues in that capacity today. This is his story.

Vic's grandfather, Frederick A. Henningsen, immigrated to the U.S. from Denmark in 1882 with his wife, Agnes Paulsen, and ten children. Frederick founded the company and two more children were born in the U.S., one being Vic's father. The family originally settled in Denver, Colorado, but on purchasing a creamery in Superior, Nebraska moved there and formed Henningsen Produce Company in 1889. The business grew rapidly and plants opened in Butte, Montana; Portland, Oregon; Shanghai, China, with other facilities throughout the Midwest and Far West.

Vic was born on May 19,1924 in New York City, the son of Victor W. Henningsen and Muriel Ann Dillion Henningsen. The family lived in Pelham Manor, New York and Vic continues to live in that community with his wife of 56 years, Mayde Ludington. His early years included Pelham Public School, Phillips Academy in Andover, Massachusetts, the U.S. Merchant Marine Academy where he later served as midshipman in maritime service on active duty in the Atlantic, Pacific, Mediterranean and Indian Ocean war zones from 1943-46. Vic was commissioned as Lt. (J.C.) U.S. Navy and served in the reserves until 1949. In 1950 he graduated from Yale University with a Bachelor of Arts in Economics and a Bachelor of Science from Kings Point. Vic entered the business full time in 1950, after having spent his summers working in the New York office and the plant in Lamesa, Texas.

Over the years, Vic has seen many technological advances such as in processing egg solids, dehydrating poultry meat, the mechanization of egg breaking, and improved spray-drying techniques. He also witnessed the improved functionality of egg products with the stabilization of egg solids to improve shelf life and preserve flavor.

Yet with the new technologies and improved product development, Vic lamented how the economics of supply and demand were lessons never fully grasped by the industry. He recalls how the USDA had created an advisory panel to smooth out the sharp production discrepancies. Vic served on that panel to help forecast and recommend early warnings, but consumer advocates charged the panel was "price fixing" and so it was abandoned.

Vic has many fond memories, beginning with his first paycheck. The greatest, however, was the Centennial Celebration of the company.

He remembers both friend and competitor coming together for that celebration, underscoring the collegiality. People that stick out in Vic's mind are Dr. George Stewart, technical advisor from 1937 to the mid-70s when he retired. George was professor and chairman of the Food Technology Department at Iowa State, and under his guidance, Henningsen's began a research and development program that improved the laboratories and quality control, helping the company become world leaders in the production and marketing of egg solids.

Vic was active in the national associations and recalls the days of the Poultry & Egg Institute of America. The Egg Solids Committee was formed under the Institute. When it ended, USDA's Connor Kennett encouraged the development of a new organization. Thus, United Egg Association was formed and continues to serve the egg products industry well. Vic also credits the American Egg Board and United Egg Producers with guiding the industry extremely well.

What does he recommend for the incoming generation of people in the egg industry? Follow George Santayanas who said, "He who ignores history is doomed to repeat it." Vic added that one should build to your market using proven economic principles. He encourages research and development. Don't depend on windfall profits. Be active in your trade associations. Lastly, be a competitor, not an enemy.

Judging from the success that Vic Henningsen has enjoyed, and how truly satisfied he is after 81 years of living, we strongly suggest we all follow his advice.

EDWARD F. HOERNING, former Laboratory Manager, USDA, AMS, Science & Technology Programs, Gastonia, NC.

Today, it is someone you see at every egg products plant in the U.S.; the federal inspector making sure the plant operations

conform to the regulations and procedures of the Egg Products Inspection Act (EPIA) of 1970. The EPIA requires mandatory USDA inspection of all liquid, frozen and dried egg product processing. EPIA also defines "restricted shell eggs" and designates them to be processed at inspected USDA plants or classified as inedible product. Prior to this law, egg products processing was a secondary industry to the shell egg producer/packers. It served as a salvage outlet for under grade shell eggs. Many processors relied on hand breaking and were low volume producers of egg products. There were some major processors of egg products prior to 1970, and they were concentrated in the Midwestern U.S., a considerable distance from the major population areas.

Those who were in the egg products industry in the early 70s know that the passage of the Egg Products Inspection Act had a monumental impact that is still felt today more than three decades later. Federal inspection enhanced product safety and wholesomeness while providing a level playing field for the processors through the uniform application of the requirements under the EPIA. This was also a huge undertaking.

Ed Hoerning was one of the original twelve USDA supervisory egg product inspectors throughout the U.S. given the task of applying uniformly the EPIA and the regulations and procedures that were part of the inspection requirements. Being a part of the USDA team that implemented the EPIA, Ed had interaction with just about every egg products producer in the northeastern U.S. Many of those plants eventually qualified for USDA inspection. In 1971-72 Ed conducted the training of approximately 100 new USDA egg products inspectors as part of the EPIA implementation process. The main training sites were at UC-Riverside, Riverside, CA and at Rutgers University, New Brunswick, NJ.

When Ed started with USDA, frozen egg products were almost exclusively packaged in metal 30 lb. containers. This was the standard. During Ed's career he has seen everything from consumer sized containers to bulk tanker shipments of liquid egg products and every type package in between for marketing egg products. After 42 years with USDA working with the egg products industry, Ed Hoerning retired on

July 1, 2005. During those years, Ed had the opportunity to survey over 50 plants to determine if they met USDA standards. He traveled extensively throughout the U.S. and Puerto Rico to review egg products facilities and trained hundreds of USDA inspectors. He managed the USDA laboratory and had oversight on testing samples from just about every egg products plant in the U.S. His is a familiar face to the egg products industry and his contributions serve all as a reminder that industry and government can effect change for the better of all Americans.

Ed Hoerning knew poultry and eggs early in his life, having grown up on a small family poultry farm in the Hudson Valley of New York State. He graduated from Cornell University with a major in Poultry Science. In 1963 Ed joined USDA, AMS and was assigned to the New York City Poultry Grading Office. It was with USDA that he performed grading work on shell eggs and poultry. The same year he began various assignments performing the inspection of egg products. In the latter part of 1963, he started the first laboratory testing services offered by USDA for egg products in New York City. The lab was closed in 1976 and relocated to Gastonia, NC where today its staff of 40 is a multi-agricultural commodity testing laboratory servicing the various food industries as well as the U.S. egg products industry. The USDA laboratory offers microbiological, chemical and physical testing for these industries.

Ed Hoerning remembers the many people who played a role in shaping his career and contributions to the egg products industry. USDA personnel in the New York City and Philadelphia Poultry Grading offices had a major impact on carrying out egg products inspection responsibilities. To Ed, those who played a significant role in his life were James B.York, Henry Binnix, Joe Kopmar and Jerry Kramberg. The USDA, AMS Poultry Grading headquarters staff in Washington, D.C. set forth policy for implementation of the EPIA and maintained a successful inspection program up until 1995 when FSIS took over the responsibilities. Those individuals include: H. Connor Kennett, D. Michael Holbrook, E.I. Rosenquist, Bob Anderson, Jim Skinner, Merlin Nichols, Larry Robinson, Howard Magwire, William D. Sutherlin and Roger Glasshoff.

From the industry, Ed Hoerning says that Arthur Papetti stands out as an innovator and industry leader. Starting from very small beginnings, Arthur developed one of the world's largest liquid egg product processing companies, Papetti's Hygrade Egg Products, Inc. in Elizabeth, NJ. Over the years Arthur expanded operations in Iowa and Pennsylvania. He developed consumer sized containers, developed further processed egg products such as cooked eggs and prepared omelet mix and implemented many new processing techniques utilizing the latest models of egg breaking machines and other processing equipment. Papetti's Hygrade utilized USDA inspection when they first started processing egg products. Other industry leaders that Ed recalls from those early days include Julius Tauber, Quality Egg Products, Inc. first in Brooklyn, NY and later in Dayton, NJ. Julius expanded his business and was one of the first few companies in the northeast to have USDA inspection. The first triple tube pasteurizers were installed at his plant. Leonard Cutler, Cutler Dairy Products, Inc. Philadelphia, PA expanded his processing plant once USDA inspection was mandatory. Cutler's was one of the first companies in the northeast to produce dried egg products. They also expanded by building an additional processing plant in Alabama. At the university level, Ed remembers the contributions of Robert C. Baker, Professor of Poultry Science at Cornell University. Dr. Baker was an outstanding educator and leader in the development and research of new egg products.

Ed Hoerning's words of wisdom to new USDA inspectors: "Listen to the management of egg products plants for their concerns and efforts on producing wholesome product. Be practical and use common sense in carrying out inspection duties." Finally, in Ed's book, there are only two "grades" of egg products. There are good eggs and bad eggs. In our book Ed, you are definitely a "good egg."

Dean Hughson

THE EGGMAN

He's known worldwide as "the eggman." The title fits as his golden years in sales worldwide helped catapalt

Waldbaum's sales records 600%. Dean Hughson is "the eggman."

He was born in rural Braymer, Missouri and at age 6 his family moved to Kansas City, Missouri. Dean's family had been farmers even in Canada/Ireland/Scotland before they came to the US and he was among the first generation to leave the farm.

His early years found him on the streets of Northeast Kansas City, Missouri. This was a good learning place to think fast on your feet, because if you didn't, you would get beat up... or worse. Dean enjoyed his high school days and was awarded a scholarship to Missouri Valley College in Marshall Missouri. However, his long hair and attitude didn't allow him to stay there long and so he returned to Kansas City and got a job as a typist for the City of Kansas City. Soon after he was selected to be in a training program to become a counselor/social worker. Dean worked at the City Prison every day and went to college at the city's expense, graduating from the University of Missouri-Kansas City. His training included working under one of the world's experts on Gestalt Therapy and he did group therapy and family counseling. It was a great training experience and shortly afterwards, he was promoted to City Probation Officer.

Dean learned how to quickly size up people and situations. In 1977 he moved to Fremont Nebraska to be a probation officer and an outpatient counselor for drinking drivers. Shortly thereafter he went on a blind date and ended up marrying an eggman's daughter.

One of the first questions Dr. Milton Waldbaum, his new father-in law, asked him was if he wanted to drive up with him to see his egg company. Dean knew chickens, because having been raised in the country, his family always had chickens or guinea hens around, but his first trip to Wakefield, Nebraska was an eye-opener. They had 1.6 million chickens at the time and it was a large company. It wasn't much longer after that when 'Doc' said to Dean, "Want to come to work for the company?" Dean thought, well, this is interesting, and a week later he was no longer in a suit and was standing in a chicken house learning the difference between wet and dry manure. Doc's partner, and his wife's first cousin was Dan Gardner. Dan took Dean the first day into a room and with one of his famous yellow pads drew a line and said, "Ok, you don't have to do anything if you don't want to because you are a son-in-law, but if you want to pay your own way around here you need to sell this chicken manure." It was sort of a challenge and Dean liked it. Within a few months he had all of the manure sold (200 tons/day on a dry basis) and they promoted him to selling inedible egg powder, which was a major problem in those days. Waldbaum's had a warehouse full of inedible which was sold to pet food companies. The second sales call Dean ever made resulted in a million pound sale. Quickly, Doc and Dan decided Dean was going to learn the egg products business.

Dean credits much of his success to his mentors like Doc and Dan. When you have mentors like those two men your learning curve is fast. One day Dan said to Dean, "What do you know about Europe?" Dean replied, "Nothing." Dan said, "Ok, go to Europe and find out what we have to do to sell products." Imagine how amazing it was to be a young man with an American Express card heading out to France, Germany, UK, Sweden, Italy, Holland and learning the egg business from first class hotels. No matter where he was, every day he called and talked to Doc for one or two hours.

Dean had three little kids at home while he was juggling the life of a busy eggman. Every morning he would get up and, rain or shine, drive from Sioux City, Iowa to Wakefield, Nebraska. Dean always favored big station wagons to "bust through" the three-foot snow drifts and many days he would make it to work when Wakefield people were calling in to report they couldn't get there. Dean would then go and pick them up.

Dean was allowed to sit in all of the meetings and got to hear the planning sessions of Doc and Dan but also got to meet the leaders in the industry: people like Goodwin Sonstegard, Lenny Ballas, Harold Cutler, the Schneider brothers, David Weiner, The Papetti Brothers, Tom Rechsteiner, Jerry Sheridan, Blair Van Zetten, Fred Adams, Dick Vogel, Mel Kriegel, Phil Sonstegard, Gil Eckhoff, Morten and Torben Ernst, Terry Ames, Dick Downs, Vic Henningsen Jr., Hugh Wiebe, Elliot Gibber, Michael Shevi, Bob Sparboe, Don Paulsen, Norm Thompson, Larry Pemberton, Roy Mosier, Stan Williams . . . the list could go on

forever. Dan got Dean involved in the business relationships with Japan and Dean made many trips to Tokyo and negotiated multi-million dollar deals, which was not a normal experience for young men. Dan got Dean involved in the International Egg Commission and United Egg Producers. He got to work with people like Al Pope, Greg Murch, Ken Klippen, and Lou Raffel and saw what associations can do for the industry. One thing he quickly learned was how important the USDA was and people like Frank Santo, Ralph Swearingen and Conner Kennett were Dean's "teachers." Dean's knowledge grew from his associations with USDA plant people like Roger Glasshoff, Howard Magwire, Darrell Wagner, and later, Marshall Thibodeaux. His trips to Washington would result in his learning how to lobby Senators and Congressional staff and understand the political process.

Dean was able to participate in what may have been the 'golden age' of egg products. Some of the experiences he had were amazing. For instance, the CIA had Dean 'help' a friend of the U.S. government in the Middle East. Here he got to visit the Pyramids at 1 a.m. in the morning and was offered a dance with a very famous dancer, which he declined due to shyness. During that visit they took Dean to lunch and while eating his pigeon in rice, 37 midgets popped up out of a stage and were singing "You Don't Bring Me Flowers Anymore."

Dutifully, Dean would write a fax to Dan each night. At times Dean felt sure that Dan must have thought he was crazy during that trip. Dean ended up being airlifted out of Egypt and going to an eggman's house in France to recover from a near death health experience from eating raw sushi with the Chief Supreme Court Justice and the Chief of Police of Egypt. Doc and Dan never questioned Dean; just asked if he learned something, and he always did. One trip, again on behalf of the U.S. government, Dean found himself lying on the bottom of a CIA plane as they went in for a quick fill up of gas in Panama. They were shooting on the runway. Dean could only imagine his kids telling people, "My father was killed selling eggs in South America on a CIA plane."

Dan's sons, Kirk and David, and Dean had fun working together. His co-workers included Butch Utemark, Dick Brownell, Don Paulsen, Dallas Roberts, Mike Loofe, Tim Bebee, Phil Rouse, and Bob Penn.

Many of the friends Dean made in those days remain his closest friends today. In 1987 he was elected Chairman of the United Egg Association Further Processors Divison, which was a very big honor for a young man.

Dean helped drive the company from $20 million a year when he began to $122 million a year when they sold it.
But all good things come to an end and, with Doc's health failing quickly, they sold the company. It was never the same again working for the people who bought you out. Dean quit and did charity projects during his non-compete days. His international experience came in handy when he went over and set up an underground communication system for Russian Jews who were being refused exit visas and Dean had to outrun the KGB.

Dean survived a divorce. Through a customer in Mexico City he met his second wife, Yoly, and remains married to her today.

Dean was working for Arthur and Tony Papetti and Tom Rechsteiner, helping them buy Monark Egg in Kansas City. Dean was President of the Company. Few people get the opportunity to study under 'masters' like those guys. In 1993 he decided to go to work for himself and again did charity work during a non-compete period, bringing free health care to Mexico.

Since 1996 Dean has been involved in helping companies worldwide on a wide range of projects including upgrading the egg products industry in Mexico and helping train new leaders in the egg industry. He feels fortunate for having friends like Phil Sonstegard, Frank Selph Sr., Jim Hull, Hugh Wiebe, Cesar de Anda, Ignacio Castillo, and Mark Campbell, who were customers as well as friends all these 'later years'. Through it all, Dean has been an eggman and while he does many other things, including writing for newspapers and consulting on healthcare, including helping recruit nurses from Central America and developing an English school, he is quite content being known as an eggman. Today Dean runs a listserv discussion group for egg people and happily he sees new people coming into this industry that he loves. He hopes they get the opportunities he had to see the world, make friends, and sell the incredible food product, eggs. Further, he hopes they have some adventures because it helps in many other ways. His three kids are all grown up and won't be in the egg business but they know their grandfather and father were. For you see, Dean is THE EGGMAN and he's still proud of it.

Dean and Yoly Hughson reside in Fountain Hills Arizona. He maintains his website at www,eggman.cc/ and is a consultant in the egg industry worldwide.

Joanne Ivy

She's the "first lady" in representing the U.S. egg industry, and is recognized internationally for her passion and commitment in promoting eggs and egg products. Yet among the many egg producers and processors worldwide who know and respect Joanne Ivy, she's really the "queen of egg promotion." After 30 years in the egg industry, Joanne Ivy, Senior Vice President with the American Egg Board, says she loves her job, and looks forward to each day "egg-cited" about the new opportunities to promote eggs.

Joanne's first position in the egg industry was with the North Carolina Department of Agriculture (NCDA) as a marketing specialist. Her responsibilities included a special emphasis of promoting North Carolina's poultry industry. In 1977, she became the executive director of the North Carolina Egg Association, and continued in that position for nine years. In 1986, she joined the American Egg Board (AEB) as Director of Industry Relations. In 1988, Joanne was promoted to Vice President. Her responsibilities were expanded to include AEB's administration and assessment collection programs, as well as providing direction for the industry relations activities. During this period, she organized an aggressive nationwide producer communications campaign (creating a grassroots network) to inform egg producers of the benefits of the American Egg Board. Her motivation in creating this network was the belief that an "Informed Producer is a Supportive Producer." The result of Joanne's efforts speaks volumes. National referendums were passed to increase the AEB assessment to an effective marketing level and to make the assessment mandatory — a cost of production for all producers. In 1996, Joanne was promoted to Senior Vice President. In this current position, she continues all of her previous responsibilities, but also handles the areas of egg product market development, retail merchandising, and export marketing. At that time, the Egg Product Marketing Program was basically non-existent, so there were great opportunities to develop a comprehensive, effective marketing program. Joanne was up to the challenge.

The first step in creating this marketing (and research) program was the establishment of a Food Technology Advisory Council. This group (university food scientists, R & D and Marketers of food manufacturers and bakers, nutrition and food safety experts) are among the "best minds" and expertise in the marketing of egg products. They meet annually to provide vital input and direction into the development of the American Egg Board's program.

Joanne is recognized globally through her involvement in the International Egg Commission. She currently serve as an officer, she's on the executive committee, and is chairman of the Marketing Committee. In addition, she has provided marketing assistance to the Egg Processors International (EPI) (IEC's further processor organization.)

Joanne's contributions to the world's egg industry received acclaim at the 2005 International Egg Commission Annual Conference in Amsterdam, where she received the organization's highest honor; the Denis Wellstead Memorial Trophy as "The International Egg Person of the Year." Upon receiving this most prestigious award, Joanne said, "I feel very humbled, yet flattered and privileged to receive this award." Joanne also serves as AEB's liaison to the United Egg Association, which represents the U.S. further processors, and to the USA Poultry & Egg Export Council, which promotes the exporting of eggs and egg products.

Joanne Ivy received her Bachelor of Science degree from Old Dominion University in Norfolk, VA. In 1992, she earned the Certified Association Executive (CAE) designation of the American Society of Association Executives.

Not many people can say they love their job with the same passion and dedication that Joanne Ivy does. Her contributions to the promotion of eggs and egg products are unsurpassed by anyone. She truly is a Queen!

Bob Kellert

Bender Goodman Co., Inc.

Jersey City, New Jersey

Few people in the egg industry understand the nuances of egg brokering like Bob Kellert. His background of 12 years working on Wall Street, coupled with his education of a Bachelor of Arts degree in economics and finance, means Bob understands brokering, so when he was invited into the family business by his father-in-law, he thought he knew all that was needed to know. But this industry is dynamic and ever changing and everyone in it soon learns the need for adjustments. Changes have occurred in Bob's tenure in the business too. He has seen the decline in frozen eggs with the growth in liquid and dried egg products. He has endured continued shrinkage in customers through mergers, acquisitions and failures (bankruptcies, etc.). He has experienced more competition for remaining customers and more predatory pricing. The business now involves dealing with professional buyers instead of "someone off the floor," electronic auctions for products and increased paperwork on all divisions. Bob has seen it all and endured it. The most significant changes he says is the decline in the customer solvency and the shrinkage in their numbers. Bob keeps on working in this business along with his father-in-law, who continues to be involved partially after more than 60 years in the business.

He remembers with fondness the good moments in his career, like watching his first load of liquid egg being delivered to a new customer in the 70s. It's also the people who add so much to a satisfying career. Bob credits many, but especially Shepard Shaff, Joe Talcott, Neil MacEwen, Arthur and Tony Papetti, Fred Adams, and Tom Rechsteiner.

What would he like to see changed? A greater understanding by the customers of costs and more intelligent packers who stop using predatory pricing to get customers who won't "remember in the morning." He also feels that more consolidation is needed, as well as still greater control over raw material sources. He anticipates more departures and consolidations in the future. Bob notes that the economics are not favorable and he expects many customers to become financially weaker, especially the baking industry.

Bob has played an active role in trade associations, serving in the capacity of the Political Action Committee chairman for United Egg Association. He is also active in the IFT and trade organizations such as the Association for Dressings and Sauces, in which he is on several committees. He believes in the importance of trade groups to be active politically. He also credits associations with serving as a clearing house for industry problems and consolidating a united voice to the outside world, as well as educating the various governmental agencies.

What would Bob recommend for the incoming generation of people? "Get a strong technical and economics background. Learn about your cost structure and support your associations and their lobbyists," said Bob. That recommendation well supports what Bob has done as well. He certainly is a good example for others to follow.

CONNOR KENNETT, JR.

His voice intonation coupled with his North Carolina accent may have led some to believe this former USDA administrator was a "pushover", but anyone dealing with Connor Kennett knew his soft-spoken nature had the force of a smithy's hammer on an anvil. He came from the broiler industry before joining USDA in 1956. In the late 60s and early 70s, Connor became a familiar voice among the egg industry while he helped develop the Egg Products Inspection Act, and the Egg Research and Consumer Information Act.

Connor understood poultry, having been raised growing broilers and working in the processing plants of Durham, North Carolina. His BS degrees from NC State in Poultry Science contributed to his positions of progressive responsibility at USDA. He served as the director of the Agricultural Marketing Service Poultry Division from 1973 to 1988 when he retired and moved to Sanford, North Carolina with his wife, Aldith.

Connor recalls the implementation of a mandatory inspection program for eggs. Under the old voluntary inspection program, USDA had been inspecting less than 100 plants producing about 80% of the liquid, frozen and dried product. These plants had to meet certain requirements for raw material used, meet required facility and sanitary standards, and conduct operations in accordance with federal regulations, including pasteurization, to meet the voluntary standards. Converting these plants over to a mandatory program was fairly easy, but the 750 other egg breaking operations ceased operations on or about July 1, 1971 (after the Egg Products Inspection Act was signed into law). In June, 1976, there were 142 official egg products plants, operating 163 shifts under inspection, staffed by 166 resident inspectors (114 federal and 52 state employees). Another provision in the Egg Products Inspection Act was the prohibition of imports of egg products from foreign countries which do not have inspection systems substantially equivalent to the U.S. system. The shell egg provisions of the Act dealt with undergrades or restricted eggs including checks, dirties, incubator rejects, inedible, leakers and loss. To determine compliance in not using these eggs for human food, egg packing stations and hatcheries had to be inspected quarterly. These inspections were also extended to the food institutions to make sure no restricted eggs were being used. Violations were usually minor infractions dealing with irregularities such as incomplete records or labeling infractions. Other violations were dealt with more severely. That was when Connor's hammer came down on the anvil. The result of the law and enforcement was responsible, at least partly, with the drop in the incidence of Salmonella food poisoning traced to contaminated eggs.

Among Connor's crowning achievements is the Egg Products Inspection Act. He cited the success of this legislation with the cooperative spirit of the industry, coupled with a good attitude at USDA.

Among the many distinctions awarded Connor was the Presidential Award for "Meritorious Executive (1982), Special Appreciation Award by AEB (1977), Friend of the Year by the Maryland Egg Council (1978), Distinguished Service Award by UEP (1987), Honorary Egg Producer of the Year Award by UEP (1988), Outstanding Service Award by PEPA (1988), Good Egg Award by the NC Egg Association (1989) and the NC Hall of Fame (1997).

Anyone who knows Connor is not fooled by his soft-spoken ways and Southern accent. But it is obvious Connor is well-respected.

KEN KLIPPEN

While working on his Ph.D. at Michigan State University in 1975, Ken was invited to interview for the position of Director for Industry Relations in Washington, DC with the National Turkey Federation. The appeal of living and working in Washington, D.C. hooked Ken and he accepted the offer. In effect, he began his poultry career in Washington, D.C., and 29 years later resigned from United Egg Association in Washington, DC to pursue his consultant career. Between those 29 years, Ken has served in various capacities, including Director General of the International Egg Commission in London, England; Vice President for Procurement at American Dehydrated Foods in Springfield, Missouri; and Vice President for Eggland's Best in King of Prussia, PA. Looking back, every position has shaped his perspective on this universally dynamic industry.

His first exposure to the federal government came when he met Earl Butz, then Secretary of Agriculture for USDA under President Ford. in 1975. Washington, DC is where he wanted to be. Ken's exposure to Congress in the mid-70s was not anything like what he experienced later in the 90s. During one lunch engagement with Senator Mike Crapo from Idaho in 2004, Ken asked about the changes he had noticed over the years in the way business was conducted in the Senate. Gone were the days when Senators across the aisle practiced a decorum of courtesy and consideration. He asked Senator Crapo his explanation for the change and the Senator noted the pressures from the special interest groups were increasing in Congress all the time. Ken was representing one of those special interest groups, although he felt more like an educator than a lobbyist.

In 1975 Ken recalled a special presentation to President Ford in the White House Rose Garden. After the ceremony the invitation was extended to Ken's group for a private tour of the White House. He had to return to the car for a moment to drop off something, then ran back to catch up with the tour. A Secret Service agent stepped out from behind a bush and told Ken, "I wouldn't do that if I were you. We will yell at you once, and then we'll shoot you." That was enough of a warning to slow anyone down. It was not without foundation, because only weeks later, a man climbed the fence at the White House and was shot by the Secret Service. When Walter Mondale was serving as Vice President, Ken was walking to a meeting and saw the Vice President. After a short interview with an ABC Correspondent, the Vice President stepped forward to the crowd forming a line to shake his hand. Ken was in the crowd and thought "why not?" Earlier when Ken was traveling into Washington, D.C., he had put on his raincoat because the skies were cloudy and it looked like rain. When he got to Washington, DC, the sun had come out so he put on his sunglasses. Picture the impression Ken must have made; dark coat, sunglasses, brief case under his arm, and the fact he was watching the Secret Service agents in the crowd. By the time the Vice President reached next to Ken, someone came up behind Ken and gently pulled both of his elbows backward and said "excuse me". The natural thing to do was turn around to see why someone was excusing himself. No one was there. When Ken turned back to shake the Vice President's hand, he saw several Secret Service agents hurrying the Vice President away. When the crowd dispersed, Ken laughed. Apparently the Secret Service had picked out Ken as suspicious judging from his appearance.

When Ken returned to Washington, D.C. in 1999, he met with many members of Congress and some he considered goodhearted people. This included Rep. Jack Kingston from Georgia, who did his level best to help the poultry industry. When Ken was having lunch in his office with Rep. Kingston, he told him he was retiring from the egg industry. The Congressman looked at him and said, "How can you, Ken. At 54, you are too young to retire." Ken's response was he was not leaving altogether, just leaving Washington, D.C. He didn't elaborate to the Congressman that he saw federal funds being spent on pork barrel projects and that turned his stomach. It didn't matter which political party spent the money, it was the principle of spending to garner support for incumbents getting re-elected. When he listened to a Congressional staffer explain that a Congressman's number one priority was to get re-elected, Ken concluded it was time for him to leave. While working in Washington, D.C., Ken spoke highly of the people he worked with and their professionalism, including Randy Green, Mike McLeod, Laura Phelps in the law firm of McLeod, Watkinson and Miller. He enjoyed working with Drs. Don McNamara and Hilary Shallo Thesmar and all the staff at the Egg Nutrition Center. He also spoke highly of the other poultry associations in Washington, D.C. and their leaders, including George Watts and Bill Roenigk at the National Chicken Council and Alice Johnson at the National Turkey Federation. In the federal agencies, Ken developed a real friendship with many, but in particular with Judy Riggins at the USDA Food Safety and Inspection Service and Lou Carson at the Food and Drug Administration. While working on the egg safety rule during the time of the Clinton Administration, Ken remembers the bumps in the road with the federal agencies on this particular rule. He remembers sitting in his office, listening to the President speak about the dangers of eating eggs, and reading the "Dear Colleague" letters going back and forth between the members of Congress showing why more regulations on the egg industry were necessary.

One day, a colleague came into Ken's office and said, "Sometimes you lose on issues. Just go on from there." Ken would not accept a loss on this one. He went in to see Mike, whose decades in D.C. gave him a realistic view on matters. Mike was not hopeful of success. Knowing the situation looked dim, Ken gambled and invited a representative from the consumer organizations proposing stricter regulations on the egg industry. That representative was Rich Wood with the Food Animal Concerns Trust (FACT). Rich flew into Washington, D.C. from Chicago and met privately with Ken in his office.

"What do you want, Rich?" was Ken's opening sentence. The consumer groups wanted the egg industry to test for Salmonella. If any Salmonella was found in the environment, then Rich wanted all the eggs from that farm to be pasteurized. Ken reasoned with Rich that testing the environment for Salmonella and then diverted eggs simply because Salmonella was discovered on the farm would be an undue burden. Ken said the industry wanted to produce a safe and wholesome product. Ken suggested a compromise that eggs be diverted to pasteurization when a positive "egg" sample was found. After all, the egg industry was selling eggs, not their poultry environments to consumers. Rich agreed to the compromise and convinced the other six consumer groups.

When FSIS, FDA and the staff for the Congressional offices all met in Ken's office to register the compromise, the egg safety rule moved forward. Judy Riggins came over to Ken to congratulate the industry on the compromise and to say, "This is how government and industry are supposed to work together." It was a proud moment in Ken's career.

In his consultancy, Ken has enjoyed the experience of helping the Iraq Poultry Producers Association build their infrastructure. When Ken was invited to Cairo, Egypt to meet with the Iraqis, he jumped at the opportunity. A few days before the group met in Egypt, one of the Iraqis who had planned to attend was murdered in his home. The group moved forward nonetheless, demonstrating their determination to rebuild amidst the war in and around Baghdad. Ken explained to the Iraqis some of the benefits of associations. He spoke highly of the continuing education in new technology and invited the group to Atlanta to attend the International Poultry Exposition. They applied for their visas immediately and two months later were traveling to the U.S. to see the show. As Ken introduced the group to the poultry leaders from the U.S., he recalls how he introduced Al Pope as his mentor and the one person who has done more to help shape Ken's career. Those words touched Al's heart and he responded emotionally. Al and Ken worked as a team for nearly 16 years and in other capacities for 7 years. Leaving UEP and UEA was hard for Ken, but leaving Al was even harder. Ken's health was being jeopardized by the continuing stresses in Washington, D.C., so he chose to start off on a new career. Every step he's taken has been both interesting and a learning experience. This includes writing this book, along with Art Papetti and Dean Hughson. The person Ken credits with giving him support and encouragement throughout his varied career is his wife, Patricia. They live in Eastern Pennsylvania near their daughter, Lara, and her husband, Jamie. Family means a great deal to Ken, and those who know him know that fact too.

BORGE KORSGAARD, Managing Director, Sanovo International

Odense, Denmark

At international meetings of egg processors, it's easy to spot Borge Korsgaard. He and his associates from Sanovo are usually in the hotel lobby, sitting around a smoke-filled table with cups of strong coffee or other beverages, negotiating deals with customers.

Borge understands the language of negotiations even when dealing with people from countries other than Denmark. Formerly he was a forwarding agent, and later became a sales manager for a trading company which included eggs. One of his good accounts was Sanovo Foods A/S. In 1989 Sanovo was searching for a managing director, and since Borge understood the business, he was the natural choice. Borge's secret for success is "learn by doing and keep a good sense of humor." His philosophy has contributed to the success of the Sanovo Group, whose owners manifest an aggressively positive way of thinking.

Things don't just happen at Sanovo; the group makes them happen. With the continuing increase in the number of eggs being further processed, coupled with the demand for more convenience foods, eggs are receiving the focus of attention by many corporations. Traditions are changing. Consumers are spending less time in the kitchen. Sanovo is positioning itself to move forward with the changes in traditions. Advancements in egg processing technology are being envisioned not only in Europe and North America, but also in Eastern Europe and the old Soviet Republics. Borge sees great possibilities for the future with the increasing globalization.

What does Borge recommend to the new generation of eggmen:

Keep both your eyes and your mind open. He says luck is needed for success, but it doesn't come automatically. You have to work hard for it. Borge and his wife, Lisbeth, have two children, a daughter Cecilie and a son, Christian.

The next time you attend an international egg meeting, look around the lobby of the hotel. You will see Borge at a table with others, smiling, negotiating, and making things happen around the world.

TIM LUBERSKI

Hidden Villa Ranch

We couldn't say that Tim was hatched into the egg business, but his parents, Edward and Aleksandra, who emigrated from Poland in the early 1940s, put Tim to work at Hidden Villa, Riverside, California, at an early age. He was stamping egg cartons at the age of 5, gathering eggs before he was 10, and then with the delivery truck drivers at the age of 11.

Tim went to school at the University of San Diego, majoring in French and mathematics. In 1976 he obtained his MBA in finance at the University of Southern California. Unfortunately, his father passed away while Tim was at USC, and Hidden Villa was sold. The love of eggs never left Tim, and he started distributing eggs from Riverside County to Los Angeles, using his apartment as an office. He purchased an egg route, recruited part-time employees from his USC fraternity and others, including his community softball team, and ran an egg distribution business. Tim is proud that he and his key managers drove Dodge Colts and Hyundais as their company cars, and boasted of paying his vendors quicker than anyone else. His level of service was also something to be proud of as his customers got product whether it was midnight or on holidays, including Christmas day when his competitors were not even answering their phones. His favorite sayings included "have fun, make money and do the right thing." Obviously this contributed to his success, for soon Tim and Hidden Villa were back in business together.

In 1983 and '84, the company was recognized by Inc 500 as one of the fastest-growing privately-owned companies. Soon Hidden Villa was trucking refrigerated eggs from the Midwest to California. Imported cheeses were added to the sales menu. In 1984, Tim bought out his largest competitor, adding supermarket customers to his foodservice customers. With the advent of food safety concerns, Hidden Villa launched a Salmonella testing program for shell eggs, claiming to be the first distributor to do so. Soon after, the dairy export division became a part of Hidden Villa, closely followed by poultry, meats, produce, soups and coffees. Before reaching his 50th birthday, Tim and Hidden Villa were selling throughout the U.S., the Pacific Rim, Mexico, South America, and the Transcaucasus area. In 1992 Tim was named Man of the Year by the City of Hope Foodservice Division. Tim works hard five days a week, and then enjoys private time with his wife and two sons on the weekend.

Mike Luker

There's a friendliness coupled with a smile that greets you when meeting with Mike Luker, president of Sunny Fresh, a division of Cargill in Monticello, Minnesota. He is genuinely affable because he truly regards the people in the egg industry as genuine.

After 30 years in the business of sales and marketing, Mike has a keen appreciation of people and knows how to make them feel at ease in his presence. He possesses all the talents of a diplomat dealing with people from other nations. That is appropriate, for he is responsible for a division of company known worldwide as a leader and innovator in foods and food products.

Mike also is known worldwide, serving as the chairman of the Egg Products International, a division of the International Egg Commission in London, England. His diplomatic skills fit well with his leadership role, both in the company he leads, as well as the international association.

Mike joined Cargill in 1990 after 15 years experience at Armour Processed Meat Company. When he came to Cargill, Mike headed up a national account sales team responsible for all of Cargill's protein divisions and the sales and marketing to many major national accounts. In 1992 he joined Sunny Fresh as their head of sales and marketing, and now he's the president. Mike received his education at the University of Arkansas and has a degree in management and labor. He actually received his degree going to night school while working full-time at Armour. There were some long days and nights but the experience and balance of the schooling and commercial experience has proven invaluable throughout his career.

Mike Luker lives in Eden Prairie, Minnesota, a beautiful suburb west of the Twin Cities of Minneapolis and St. Paul. He and his wife, Sandy, have been married for over 25 years. They met in college and dated for four years before tying the knot in May of 1980. Nine months later, they started moving around the United States, living in St. Louis, Kansas City, Omaha, Los Angeles, and then ending up in Minnesota in 1990. Mike and Sandy have three children: Mike Jr., who is 21, and a senior at Miami of Ohio, Jeff who is 17 and is a senior at Eden Prairie High School, and Jenny, who is 13 and in the 8th grade, also in Eden Prairie.

At this point, none of the family is directly involved with Sunny Fresh other than the great support they give Mike day in and day out. They do, however, help drive the per capita consumption of eggs. They are real egg-lovers!

Since most of Mike's 30 years in business have been in sales and marketing, his perspective on the egg products industry is from a sales point of view. When talking about industry issues, Mike notes how industry leaders in the past were reactionary and defensive. He envisions industry leaders being more proactive when it comes to the consumer. He readily acknowledges this is easy to say and tough to do.

Mike cites one of the best examples in the Egg Nutrition Center (ENC) and Dr. Don McNamara along with his team. Initially, ENC had to be reactionary in addressing the negatives on the cholesterol issue, but today it is very proactive with great results, both in the United States and globally.

As to the future, Mike anticipates many challenges for the industry as it moves through the 21st century. Today, the industry is focusing on Avian Influenza outbreaks and potential mutation of that virus. Globally, the EU is making moves regarding the use of cages and Eastern Europe is emerging as a global supplier of eggs and egg products. The industry is challenged with the global balance in trade and discussion of product safety, traceability, and husbandry standards. There are shifts in not only egg production but in egg marketing. Each of these challenges also represents tremendous opportunities for the industry and U.S. producers and marketers. Mike foresees great opportunities for the industry to continue to provide leadership in the U.S. as well as the evolving global marketplace.

Mike is proud of the egg products industry and the people who helped shape it. He's quick to credit people like Fred Adams, Bob Sparboe, Dan Gardner, Arthur Papetti, Al Pope, Dennis Casey and Harry Herbruck. He gives high marks to Jerry Rose, who served as president of Sunny Fresh Foods from 1988-2000 and who is now in a senior leadership role with Cargill. Jerry continues to be one of their best egg salespersons, never missing an opportunity to always ask whomever he is addressing whether they had eggs for breakfast or not. He's also proud of the people from Sunny Fresh including Warren Johnson, Terry Profit, and the entire Sunny Fresh team which has now grown to well over 500 stakeholders who really care about the business, care about the industry, care about each other and care about the customer.

What does Mike recommend for the incoming generation of people into the egg products business? Never lose sight of the marketplace. Focus your efforts on the consumer. Face the challenges, be aggressive and sensitive to the changing needs of the marketplace.

We'd like to add a few more from Mike's own example. Learn to

develop diplomatic skills, be quick to put a smile on your face, and accept people in this industry as genuine. They really are the best!

Don McNamara

If the entire world were polled and asked who has done more for increasing the consumption of eggs and egg products, they would have to answer Dr. Don McNamara, executive director of the Egg Nutrition Center, Washington, DC.

Don became involved with the egg industry as a scientific advisor on the cholesterol issue. He was a member of the first American Egg Board – Egg Nutrition Center Scientific Advisory Panel and served from 1984 to 1990 and again between '92 and '95. In 1995 he accepted his current position as executive director of the Egg Nutrition Center.

Don started working in cholesterol research in 1966 as a doctoral student in the Department of Biochemistry at Purdue University. Almost forty years later he acknowledges he's still learning about cholesterol, nutrition, health and eggs. From 1966 to 1995 he spent time at Purdue University (PhD 1972), Ohio State University Medical College (NCI Post-doctoral Fellow, 1972-74), Rockefeller University (assistant professor, 1974-1980); associate professor, 1980-1985) and the University of Arizona (professor of nutritional sciences, 1985-1995). During those years his primary research area dealt with the effects of dietary lipids, fatty acids and cholesterol, the regulation of cholesterol and lipoprotein metabolism as related to atheriosclerosis and the risk of heart disease. Today that experience is used to educate health professionals and the public on the role of eggs in a healthy diet.

It is a common axiom to say that behind every successful man there is a supporting wife. This is especially true with Don. He is married to Rosa, who helps him is in promoting eggs and the Egg Nutrition Center, both in the USA and internationally. She is a great supporter of the industry and her language skills continue to be of great benefit to Don. She also understands why Don is often asked to speak at conferences around the world, and so is away on extended business trips. Rosa keeps occupied on those ventures with her own interests in horticulture.

Don believes that one of the biggest changes in the industry has been the change in attitude regarding the health effects of dietary cholesterol and eggs. The lifting of the "no more than 3 to 4 whole eggs a week" by the American Heart Association has resulted in a significant change in the opinions of both the public and health professionals. There is still room for improvements, such as the lifting of the dietary guideline to limit cholesterol intake to "no more than 300 milligrams per day." This would have a huge impact on the industry.

Would Don do it all over again? To leave a tenured professorship at a research university to work for a commodity group was a major decision and was not taken lightly, said Don. He added that he has not regretted that decision, and has found the experience to be challenging, gratifying and rewarding at many levels – as a scientist, as an educator and as a mentor.

Concerning the future, there is a wealth of opportunity in the industry to expand the nutritional benefits of eggs, including enhanced nutrient-enriched shell eggs and modified egg products. Don believes that over time, eggs will play a major role as a natural source of many essential and functional nutrients.

Among Don's most memorable experiences was when Al Pope offered him the position as executive director of the Egg Nutrition Center. Don knew that if he accepted, there would be major changes in his life. The first change was returning to Tucson and asking Rosa to marry him. After twenty years of being single, that was a memorable experience.

When it comes to people who have impacted Don's life, he cannot sufficiently express his gratitude to, and appreciation of, Al Pope, President of United Egg Producers. "As a boss," Don says, "he has the personality and management skills which make my job so much easier. As a friend, he is someone I can always count on for encouragement and support. I've worked with Jani Aronow for over twenty years and she has been an exceptional colleague over those years as she transforms science speak to media sound bites. Lou Raffel and Joanne Ivy of the American Egg Board have consistently provided their support and valuable insights on the functioning of a commodity research and promotion program. And last, but certainly not least, the past and current staff of the Egg Nutrition Center, who have worked so very hard to make me look good and to get out the good news about eggs."

When it comes to trade associations and their impact on the industry, Don says that the producer funded program is indispensable in generating the research and outreach dollars so important to the success of the Egg Nutrition Center. Without the research, there would never have been a change in the American Heart Association's egg restrictions or in our ability to promote eggs for their many positive nutritional contributions to the American diet. The producer dollars fund the research and fund getting those research findings to the health community.

What would Don recommend to the next generation of people in the egg industry? To take confidence in the fact that they are producing a nutritious and healthy product, that its contributions to the nutritional well-being covers the entire human lifespan, and that their support of the American Egg Board and Egg Nutrition Center is an essential component of a successful business.

Don, it's leaders like you who inspire our confidence. Your legacy is ensured as one who did more for the industry worldwide than can be expressed in this story. Thank you, Don!

JULIAN MADELEY

He's probably the youngest egg industry association executive in the world, but he's risen to the top post of leading the world's egg industries. His skills in communication, coupled with a comprehension of issue management internationally, have catapulted this young executive into a world leader.

Julian Madeley is currently Director General of the International Egg Commission (IEC) headquartered in London, England. The IEC is the global voice of the world's egg producers and further egg processors, and is the only organization that represents the world's top egg industry decision-makers in over 50 countries. The IEC plays an important role in representing its members at global bodies such as the OIE (the World Animal Health Body), Codex Alimentarius and the World Trade Organization (WTO). Julian took on his role at the IEC in 2003, after gaining experience of the egg industry around the world. He trained as a lobbyist working for United Egg Producers at McLeod, Watkinson & Miller law firm in Washington D.C., with the team representing the American egg industry to the U.S. government. He then went on to become a lobbyist with the British Egg Industry Council in London, working on the passage of the European Welfare Directive into U.K. domestic law and to have input into the WTO negotiations. This position gave him an understanding of not only domestic government in the U.K., but also enabled him to work with the European Commission in Brussels and the World Trade Organization in Geneva.

His experiences are not limited to the U.S. and the U.K. Julian has also had the opportunity to work in South Central Africa with egg production on both a commercial level and developmental level for refugee camps. He spent time working in Southeast Asia, completing an economic study for a major UK clearing bank.

Julian was brought up working in the family egg production and marketing business and has a firsthand knowledge of the industry. This was further developed, including time spent with alternative egg production systems and pullet rearing, while working for Lloyds Animal Feeds, a U.K. national producer of eggs and feedstuffs.

Julian was educated at Corpus Christi College, Cambridge, gaining a first class master of Philosophy Degree in economics and finance. He had previously studied general agriculture at Harper Adams University College.

Julian was awarded a Nuffield Farming Scholarship in 1997, allowing him to travel extensively for three months looking at the egg industry in North America. Since then, he has been an active member of the Nuffield Poultry Study Group, traveling to Mexico, Brazil, China and Poland.

Julian is still directly involved with the family business with his parents and sister Nichola. The business is evolving from its farming roots to encompass residential property development and event organization, although egg production and marketing are still at the heart of daily life.

Julian says he has benefited tremendously from all the support and guidance from many people in the egg industry. He believes that the egg industry is extremely rewarding, and is run by a truly unique set of individuals, who make participation in this industry a real honor. We agree with Julian, only he's a significant part of that leadership and in working with him is our honor and privilege.

STEVE MANTON, Worldwide Egg Products, Harrogate, England

He draws comparisons in the egg business to his days racing motorcycles on the Isle of Mann where he lives off the coast of England. Steve Manton knows all about the twists and turns, bumps and scrapes of both motorcycle racing and breaking eggs. Racing was Steve's way of relaxing from his business. While racing, he had to stay focused on the ride and that helped him. Most of the time while racing motorcycles, Steve recalls the spills where he was able to get back up, dust himself off, and get right back on his bike. Not so, a few years ago when he went over a wall traveling at 125 mph. That accident nearly cost him his arm, and he spent the next five weeks staring at the ceiling from his hospital bed. One mistake in the egg breaking business can also lead to incapacity, especially when you are buying and selling eggs and egg products in 28 countries and on five continents like Steve.

Moving fast describes the life Steve has led beginning when he trained for flying jets for the RAF (Royal Air Force). Having grown up on a Yorkshire farm, he wanted to experience the world. The RAF had a program where it brought in 1000 young men and put them through the trials of flight training. Within days, the RAF had whittled the number of qualified men down to 10 and Steve was among them. He recalls the instructions to the remaining 10 men that getting through the RAF training will equip them to get through anything life throws at them. Steve learned his lessons well.

Chickens were always a part of Steve's life. His grandfather

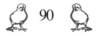

hatched chicks and sold them. Steve's father followed that same pattern. Steve broadened his horizons by selling liquid egg to a customer needing the product. Steve produced the product in an old washing machine in his garage. Those early beginnings with a few buckets of liquid egg per week soon turned into many buckets. Steve purchased a spinning machine and was cracking eggs seven days a week. He also purchased a used pasteurizer from Londegg and soon thereafter purchased an egg breaking machine. Today Worldwide Egg Products is among the leading egg breaking operations in England. They also produce inedible egg for pet foods and pigweeds from their plant in Holland.

Steve has always believed in a single market in Europe and applauds every effort to develop a global market for egg products. He feels that the EU is over-legislated and creating hardships for the manufacturing of products. If he could start over again with the energy he had when he was 20, he would begin operations in the U.S. and search for global customers. competing with the quality and the economy of U.S.-produced and processed eggs.

His energy during his 20 plus years in the business included developing a truck hauling business and a cold storage depot. He has since sold his transportation business and sold Springfield Farms, then used the money for re-investing in his business. Until he reached the age of 40, Steve only drew the money he needed to live, and then invested everything else back into the business. His philosophy is to give 110% of yourself to the business, or else, don't go into the egg business.

Steve and his wife, Debbie, have a son, Richard, and a daughter Lois. He had considered selling his business in the past, but he felt a loyalty to his longtime employees. Anyone who visits Worldwide Egg Products can easily see the mutual respect and loyalty that Steve and his employees share.

Steve is a free-thinking businessman who believes that customers should be given a choice as to the type of products they wish to buy. He participates in the British Egg Products Association and is open about his viewpoints on matters. He has worked hard to develop his business and believes that the association is best served when participants speak

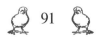

openly and freely about their viewpoints.

When recalling some fond moments in the business, Steve smiles when he remembers selling eggs into Italy for pasta manufacturing. His many trips to Italy were not just to visit customers. Steve has developed a special friendship with an Italian egg producer who inspired Steve by his willingness to take chances. The example set by his Italian friend has proven valuable to Steve's philosophy in business. Judging from the success Steve has enjoyed, we can say confidently Steve's philosophy is also an inspiration to us all.

Roy Mosier

He first started in the egg products business by working with Henningsen Foods in 1962. After working in all the Henningsen plants, Roy Mosier moved on by taking over an egg processing company in Echo Lake, Wisconsin. While looking to expand egg product sales, he found a defunct company in Topeka, Kansas called Midland Foods, a division of Seymour Foods. There wasn't much there except a couple of crudely made ovens, a spiral freezer, some conveyors, and few other items, in a warehouse, all covered with dust. The equipment at Midland had been used to manufacture IQF omelets, crepes and egg patties for the foodservice market during the 70s. It was later that McDonald's, Burger King and others were promoting breakfast, so the timing of getting equipment back and running was ideal. Roy had the plant capacity sold when they started back up. He thought himself a genius with how quickly everything was moving, so he continued with the movement by building and adding more equipment. He soon was involved with the Papettis and the Egg Specialties Company, designing commercial ovens for precooked egg products. Today, Roy is retired, but doing some part time work providing technical consulting to the industry, while his wife, Vicki, enjoys time with their daughter and nine-year-old granddaughter.

Roy recalls those years when there were only two categories of egg products; dried and frozen. Liquid sales were between breakers. The largest commercial egg-laying operation in those days was in the DeKalb tri-deck housing 6,000 chickens. In egg products, Roy recalls the intermediate step between frozen egg products and the extended shelf life products (ESL). That intermediate product was the "slush pack" held at 32-34 degrees. This was, at that time, the long life product that didn't need time to thaw.

Of all the people Roy has known in the industry, he says the Papettis were the "movers and shakers." They were aggressive marketers that kept the foodservice market growing. Roy says this is where the growth in egg products took place the last two decades. As to associations, Roy calls them "the shiny hood ornament" for working on issues like food safety.

As to the future, Roy predicts that consolidations will reduce competition, with the consumer eventually paying more. In all of this, Roy sees the opportunities for smaller, regional companies to keep the larger ones honest. He also expects to see more technical advances that will improve the functional characteristics of egg products such as those involving enzymatic processes. The most significant innovation he has seen is the development of precooked frozen egg components that are microwaveable and taste good.

Roy says the egg business has always been tough, but it has been good. He called it the "original rat race." Even if you win, you are still "a rat," says Roy. He added, it takes a real egg guy to be proud of that. Roy is proud of his accomplishments, and we're proud of him.

GREG MURCH, Senior VP, Sparboe Companies

The globalization of the egg industry began with a third generation poultryman, but he started in the turkey industry. Greg Murch was the mastermind behind the industry's export sales of shell eggs to other countries, particularly the Mideast. His contributions to this industry go beyond exports and now he works with a producer/breaker who ranks in the top five companies of the nation. His story confirms that hard work and keeping an open mind can lead to exciting and successful times in this industry.

Greg's grandfather owned and operated a vertically integrated turkey operation in Northern Wisconsin. His father, while originally involved in the family operation, spent many years involved in other turkey operations located throughout the U.S. Greg moved over to eggs when Land O'Lakes hired him to work in their Quality Egg Division. Greg's son, Aaron, is now working for Sparboe's, which will give the Murches a fourth generation of poultry industry involvement.

He grew up on a turkey farm in Northern Wisconsin. During his school years he worked on the family turkey farm but also worked for Jerome's, which later became "The Turkey Store." Greg went to college at the University of Wisconsin – River Falls, where he received a B.S. degree in broad area agriculture. He received the first Jerome Scholarship and geared his college degree towards entering the turkey industry after his graduation. During his college years he worked for the Jerome Company. He had two years of internship work and worked in every division of Jerome's at one time or another. It was disappointing that upon graduation, the turkey industry was in one of its typical bust cycles and the employment opportunities were very limited. He had a number of different offers but none that appealed to him. He was fortunate that, through his contacts in the turkey industry, he was able to secure employment with Land O' Lakes in their Quality Egg Division. Greg was hired by Gerry Weber, who, throughout his early career, served as a mentor and a good friend. As a producer service representative for LOL, Greg was able to get a broad understanding of the egg industry. LOL was involved in pullet raising, feed sales, egg production, shell egg processing and shell egg breaking. He worked with small (by today's standards) independent producers and sold production buildings, pullets and feed and purchased the eggs back from the producers. Greg was also responsible for the care and service of the pullets and layers. This broad education served Greg well in the future.

Gerry Weber left LOL, and Greg followed six months later, to work for Midwest Egg Producers. Midwest Egg Producers was an egg farmer cooperative formed to represent egg producers across the twelve Midwestern States. When Gerry took over the management of Midwest Egg Producers it was basically broke. Egg production had left the Midwest and was centered in the Southeast and on the West Coast. Under Gerry's leadership Midwest Egg Producers flourished and took a leadership position in developing new and innovative solutions to reoccurring egg industry problems. Midwest set up the first Nest Run trading program where producers could actually market their eggs, on an ongoing basis, in nest run form, and know that they were receiving a fair market value for them. Midwest was instrumental in increasing the trading on ECI to the point where the trading could represent the selling price of eggs and could be used in setting the pricing for all eggs sold. During this time, and with the participation of all of the UEP Regionals and the UEP office, the American Egg Board was initiated. The industry during this period was extremely rationalistic and protective of the producers in their own part of the United States. Very few companies spanned more that one state, let alone an entire region of the country. After five years at Midwest, Greg was invited to join the UEP office in Atlanta and head up their marketing division. It was originally intended to develop an egg carton coupon program that could be used on a nationwide basis. Unfortunately, the program was not very successful. Since he was working under the premise that he needed to make enough money for UEP to pay for his own salary, he turned to the one area that he knew something about–trading eggs. All of the UEP regionals had their own trading programs and thus Greg was only left with international markets where there was little UEP member involvement. Under the guidance of Al Pope, Greg was able to set up an export program that sold in excess of six million dollars of eggs per year. This was the first U.S. entity that sold eggs in shipload quantities around the world.

After 6 years with UEP Greg took over the management of National Egg Company, one of the six regional offices that made up the UEP Cooperative. When he took over at National Egg, they had experienced a number of bad debt losses and needed to reorganize to get their financial house in order. Through the efforts of folks like Ed Houston, Gene Southerland, Steve Rumpf, Ron Braswell, John Wallace, Fred Adams and Russ Lind, the cooperative was able to survive and take its rightful leadership position within the UEP structure. After two years with National Egg, Greg decided to go back to the "real" world and accepted a position with Crystal Farms. Crystal Farms was a Minnesota-based firm which was involved in shell egg production, processing and breaking. He was initially involved in the processing, distribution and breaking parts of the business but ultimately ended up in charge of the entire Crystal Farms Division. During his tenure at Crystal the company changed considerably and through acquisitions grew into one of the largest producers, processors and value-added businesses within the egg industry. Crystal Farms was incorporated into Michael Foods when it became a publicly owned entity. While Greg was with Michael Foods he considered himself fortunate to have been involved in the early stages of the aseptic packaging of eggs. In fact, Greg helped design and construct the first exclusive in-line breaking and aseptic packaging plant.

For the past 15 years Greg has been employed by the Sparboe Companies. He has been involved in the growth of the company as it has gone from 1.4 million to over 13 million layers today. The company entered into the further processing business with the purchases of Calmar Foods.

In Greg's 35 years in the egg business, he has seen the change to inline complexes. When he entered the industry, the concept of inline processing of eggs was just in its infancy and the idea of inline breaking had not even been considered. A second major change Greg has seen has been the growth in the value-added business. Until the 1980s less than 12% of the total eggs produced were broken. Generally, those eggs broken were only the eggs that could not be sold as graded in the shell. Today, over 33% of the eggs are broken, and entire laying complexes are dedicated to the breaking industry. Greg considers himself fortunate to have participated in both the initial stages of the aseptically packaged egg product, which is where most of the increase in utilization of liquid egg and consequently, egg products, has occurred and the advent of the inline breaking of eggs.

What would Greg like to see happen in the industry? Let those that are currently in the business stay in the business and make a reasonable return on their investment. Greg theorizes that the baggage necessary to provide that would be more onerous than the current economic system. Greg expressed concerns that the over-production in the Midwest is going to lead to the same situation the Southeast faced 25 years ago. The level of production could not be sustained, at profitable levels, and producers had to survive through extended periods of losses in order to decrease bird numbers to a point where the product could be utilized in an efficient manner.

Greg would like to see fewer outside influences in our daily activities. That may include governments, local, state and federal, do-gooders, neighbors, and non-invested third parties.

Would Greg repeat what he did in his career? He said he seemed to have been at the right place at the right time. His main mentor, Gerry Weber, afforded him the opportunity to try new and different things. He was able to associate himself with the leaders in the industry. When he needed guidance he was fortunate that there was a support system that he could utilize that willingly helped him.

Greg has been blessed with a loving and understanding wife, Linda, and his family and has been able to dedicate the time and effort needed to do his job the way he wanted to. He also had the opportunity to work with individuals that valued and rewarded independent and creative thinking. Greg is extremely proud of the fact that he reported to Gerry Weber, Al Pope, Stuart Friedell and now, Bob Sparboe. Each of these individuals were leaders, entrepreneurs and very successful in their own chosen occupations. Certainly, something from each of them rubbed off on Greg and he has become an extension of them and their thinking.

In the future, Greg sees consolidations continuing to take place. As the original entrepreneurs leave the industry, those left to manage the existing businesses will become much more professional in their approaches as to how the businesses will be run. Greg believes we will see more niche markets develop and we will see the egg products portion of our business continue to grow, although not at the rate of the past 15 years. Food safety and government intervention into our business will also continue to take a more prominent role in our decision making process. Greg expects to see some type of individual egg marking, for traceback purposes, made available. He also expects that the industry will be hit with another major disease outbreak as well as a major consumer egg safety problem. Buffers to the cyclicality of our pricing will be initiated. In the long run this will not only limit the price swings but also limit the amount of profit, as a total industry, that we will be able to make. Automation to all processes will be forced on us as labor availability becomes critical.

The most memorable occasion in Greg's career was the day they loaded the first eggs on the ship, the Playa Blanca. This was the first time that the total industry had participated in an export order. He loaded 50,000 cases directly on the ship. It would not have been as exciting if Greg hadn't had so many people tell him that it couldn't be done and that he would never get the industry to cooperate on such a venture. There was a great sense of accomplishment when they finally started loading eggs.

There are many individuals who impacted Greg's career. When he was involved in initially setting up the Nest Run trading program, the program was initiated by Gerry Weber, but without the direct involvement of Jim Rich, Fritz Graves, Bob Sparboe, Ernie Brown, Gene Gregory and Bob Hanson, the program would not have gotten off the ground. The UEP export, without the early participation and encouragement of Fred Adams, would not have been feasible.

Many in our industry do not recognize the name of Dick Olson, but without his innovative thinking and risk-taking the utilization of aseptic egg products would not have bloomed the way that it did. Likewise, the involvement of David and Doug Ford and their contribution, through North Carolina State University, to the process was essential to drive the product forward.

The concept of inline breaking, while previously done on a smaller scale, was initiated and tested by Michael Foods at their Gaylord plant. In looking at the contributions from the associations, Greg says among the issues that changed and continue to change the industry would include; increased government involvement and the industries' ability to deal with these changes, the initiation of an industry promotion program (AEB), the formation and utilization of our public trading entity (ECI) and now, the challenge that the industry faces is dealing with zealots wanting to control how producers care for the chickens.

For the incoming generation of egg people, Greg would encourage them to be innovative and creative. The industry has rewarded those who could be the best at what they do. Greg issued a warning to them that passive involvement will bring a quick exit from the industry. Those who have survived within this industry have had to commit themselves 100%. Our industry does not accept less than that and those who attempted to be less than committed are soon looking for other employment. Greg advises those who are willing to make these sacrifices to strap themselves in tight, as they are in for a "helluva ride."

Mr. Mac Ohi

QP is well known within the U.S. egg products industry and the name of the man that goes with that distinction is Mr. Ohi. After purchasing Henningsen Foods in 1990, Mr. Ohi served as the chairman for five years. In 1997, at the age of 56, he formed his own company, Agrinet International Ltd. (formerly Belovo Japan Co., Ltd.) and in 2004 the company was importing 2,300 tons of dried egg products.

Mr. Ohi understands what is involved in purchasing egg products. He started working at QP Corporation after his graduation in 1963, but it wasn't until 1975 that he got involved in eggs as the purchasing manager of shell eggs and egg products. His friendship with egg products industry around the world grew after his promotion to general manager at the purchasing department. Although he has many friends in different corners of the world, Mr. Ohi recalls fondly his time in New York with Vic Henningsen and Gil Eckhoff.

With the globalization of the egg industry, Mr. Ohi commented that many are hopeful that the IEC will provide more leadership in the egg products sector and one day there will be an international quality standard for egg products. He sees the impact that the developing countries have, but expressed concerns with the entry of India and China into the egg products industry with what may be an oversupply of product in the future.

Food safety is a primary concern of Mr. Ohi's. He pointed out

that unless those in the industry come to grips with issues like pesticide residue, antibiotics, and heavy metals, they cannot survive. He also expressed the importance of understanding Avian Influenza and the potential for a worldwide spread of this disease. Coupling the potential for oversupply, health concerns with food safety issues,
Mr. Ohi is hoping that new products will be developed in the near future. He said those who devote themselves to the future of this industry are very desirable. We can only add, people with 30 years of experience are also very desirable to the egg products industry, and that includes Mr. Ohi. There can be few people in our industry who have so many friends worldwide and Mr. Ohi has seen many eggs in his lifetime.

GREGG OSTRANDER

Trim, energetic, and with a look in his eye as if to say he knows where the buried treasure is located. Those are the first impressions when one meets Gregg Ostrander, Chief Executive Officer for Michael Foods, Inc., Minnetonka, Minnesota. His corporate office is located on the 4th floor in the impressive 301 building on the Carlson Parkway, just to the west of Minneapolis. In his office he dresses casually and exudes confidence holding the reins of the billion dollar corporation. A recently posted financial report on Michael Foods reflected an 11% gain in profits with a unit volume gain in sales of 4%. When asked how Michael Foods accomplished this feat, Gregg simply smiles. It's the same smile noted in the picture on his desk, along with his wife of 26 years, and their three boys. He commented about the Atkins diet having gone by the wayside, but the industry continues to produce shell eggs as if they know where they are going with them. Again that smile cracks the gloomy forecast for egg prices and Gregg exhales his secret: We work hard to balance how we source our eggs with how we position, price and sell our value-added egg products.

Where did this confident CEO come from? Gregg started off at Beatrice Foods in 1975, moving to president of Armour Swift Echrich Prepared Foods, a division of Con Agra, before taking the helm at Michael Foods in 1993. Gregg focused his energies and talents on marketing and general management. It was a natural progression to move from meat proteins to egg proteins for the foodservice customer base that is his company's primary target. The acquisitions that built this egg product company leader included Crystal Farms, M.G. Waldbaum, Papetti's Hygrade Eggs, and Inovatech. In 1993, the market for egg products was ramping up rapidly. Patents were developed for extended shelf life egg products. Customers were demanding consistency in pricing, but also demanded convenience, along with food safety. Michael Foods promised to deliver on all fronts, and did so. Citing specific examples, Gregg recalls how Burger King initially used shell eggs, then moved to ultrapastuerized liquid eggs and now utilizes a full-cooked egg patty in their operation. Burger King is a corporation that wants quality and consistency from its suppliers with all the assurances of food safety. Big fluctuations in product costs is not part of that corporate plan, so Michael Foods worked with their supply chain team to develop a strategy that helped smooth out pricing over a longer time horizon. This same dedication to working closely with each of Michael Foods' large customers to meet their needs, has contributed to their success.

Moving to new products and away from the commodity concept is where this industry will grow, and Gregg applauds the new designer shell eggs with Omega 3, and organic eggs. He says adding value is the dimension for consumer excitement. Gregg's leadership has added value in other ways, too. They are the largest processor in Canada and also have a joint ownership with Belovo in Belgium. The horizons for Michael Foods span the globe with sales into Japan and will one day include China. Gregg's eyes shine when he speaks about the uses for eggs in providing valuable nutrients. Who ever thought that 20 years ago eggs would become a vital link in the production and delivery of these nutrients, said Gregg.

Gregg Ostrander's most memorable experience was bringing M.G. Waldbaum and Papetti's together and making the giant that exists today. In that regard, he also spoke highly of the key individuals in that merger. The nuances of business transactions with the likes of Dan Gardner and Arthur Papetti, and then seeing this egg products corporation emerge, was something Gregg will never forget.

Gregg sees the value of trade associations, but prefers his low-key approach with staff involvement instead of himself. He is proud of the leadership Toby Catherman has provided the United Egg Association, as well as the contributions of Terry Baker and Tim Bebee to United Egg Producers.

What would Gregg recommend for those entering the egg business? This is an exciting industry with many opportunities for young people. Be creative and dream big dreams. It is obvious Gregg has followed his own recommendations and the egg products industry has benefitted from his leadership.

Frank Pace

PACE Farm Pty. Ltd

Frank Pace is the founder and managing director of Pace Farm Pty. Ltd – Australia's foremost producer, marketer and distributor of eggs. From humble beginnings as the son of a market gardener, Frank identified a business opportunity in the egg industry. He quickly developed a reputation for quality, freshness and customer service, which led to the establishment of Pace Farm (1978).

From a 22,000 hen egg production facility, Frank's grit and determination has built Pace Farm Pty. Ltd. into 45 sites with 500 employees, 2,800,000 laying hens and an egg products processing plant. Remaining a family business, Pace Farm is Australia's market leader in egg innovation, supermarket sales and the preferred partner for food manufacturers.

Pace Farm is unique in the Australian market, offering the cost efficiencies of vertical integration and a unique corporate culture imbued with a passion for "serving the enjoyable egg." All the staff at Pace Farm reflect Frank's enthusiasm for customer service and quality produce.

Frank Pace has given more than 25 years of service to the egg industry, sitting on research and development, animal welfare and marketing committees. Despite the considerable demands on his time, he continues to provide an encouraging and steady hand to guide his four children through the challenge of divisional management within the business, while actively seeking entrepreneurial opportunities.

A visionary within the egg production industry, Frank is acutely aware of changes in customer preferences, in particular the concerns about animal welfare and the environmental impact of farming. In 2003, Frank lobbied the International Egg Commission (IEC) to adopt an international code of practice for the farming and management of layer hens. The final document has become a powerful tool for the continuation of self regulation, biosecurity and world's best practice benchmarking for the farming of layer hens. Frank's animal welfare initiatives have brought LibertyÆ Barn Laid RSPCA eggs and 100% organic eco eggs to supermarket shelves, in addition to encouraging other farmers to invest in new layer housing technology.

Frank's environmental conscience has enabled Pace Farm's $40 million West Wyalong layer investment to achieve a NSW Institute of Surveyors award for Environmental Design (2003).

"In hindsight I would have increased the speed at which I gave the children autonomy within the business. They have proved to be my greatest asset and mirror my passion and commitment. Without doubt the next generation brings a fresh set of eyes and skills to the company and I find myself becoming more and more enthusiastic about the future."

"The statutory obligations within the egg business have become increasingly complex since the industry was deregulated. We're seeing increasing consolidation and pressure from government departments, welfare groups and industry bodies to improve producer practices and accountability. In this climate of corporate governance it's a natural evolution to invest in emerging technology. At Pace Farm we have invested significantly in the new layer housing technology, grading floor machinery and software to manage resources and products across our 45 locations. At the press of a button I can see the production levels of flocks

800 kilometres away; or log onto the internet to see where all our trucks are on the road."

"I believe that society will divide into two distinct groups – one group that embraces the speed of corporate life and purchases pre-prepared and restaurant foods; and a second group that yearns for the simple pleasures of cracking open the shell of a fresh egg, home cooking and family. As a businessman, I'm placing a bet both ways."

Frank has a history of achievement. He is one of five board members of Australia's peak egg industry marketing body, Australian Egg Corporation Ltd.; was afforded the honour of being made one of only four of the Commission's Office Bearers (2002) and Vice-Chairman (2005).

His personal honors include being awarded a life membership and Paul Harris Fellow with the Rotary Club of Mount Druitt; the Crystal Egg Award (IEC global marketing award) for the launch of Liberty Æ Barn Laid RSPCA eggs; and the Denis Wellstead Memorial Trophy for "International Egg Person of the Year" (2005). Frank was previously the Chairman of the Seven Hills branch of the former Livestock and Grain Producers Association (LGPA) and a member of the NSW Farmers' Association Egg Committee.

"The most memorable experience I have had in the egg industry was being awarded the Denis Wellstead Memorial Trophy. The emotion of being applauded and acknowledged by your peers is truly overwhelming. I was both humbled and proud, and felt blessed that my family could share that moment with me."

A philanthropic supporter of Variety Club Children's Charity, scientific research, the Firefighter's Association and cancer research, Frank Pace has a lifelong history of active contribution to the local community. "My wife has been the greatest source of inspiration for the Pace Farm brand and community face of this business. Life gives you many lessons and challenges - we almost lost our first home to fire, our family was touched by cancer and we have always felt strongly about helping disabled and disadvantaged children. Diana has certainly taught me that if you have a strong corporate image, underpinned by community involvement, then customers will want to buy your product and the best people will want to work for you."

"My recommendation for the new generation of egg producers is to have a vision, passion and commitment to what you do. To share with and learn from other people, to get involved with your local trade and industry associations, because you don't need to re-invent the learning curve for your business. To give back, because that's the only way you can truly be rewarded."

ARTHUR PAPETTI

Papetti's Hygrade Egg Products, Inc.

Elizabeth, New Jersey

The egg products industry worldwide has many innovative and forward-thinking businessmen. Many are leaders that help chart the course of the entire industry through their participation in their national and international associations. Many are savvy in marketing and are able to lead their companies to profitable results. But few truly possess the wisdom that have taken concepts, both in technology and marketing, and created a dynasty recognized around the world.

The Papetti family has achieved this world recognition for their wisdom in bringing to the egg products industry new concepts and new ideas that catapulted egg products to the forefront of the institutional and retail customers. Two brothers, Arthur and Anthony (Tony), helped shape the dynasty known as Papetti's Hygrade Egg Products, Inc., which ended up employing nearly 900 people in five states–New Jersey, New York, Pennsylvania, Iowa, and Missouri–and producing nearly fifty different egg products and one hundred twenty different items from an egg for institutional and retail buyers. Arthur became the company president and was the industry representative and Tony served as company controller and chairman. The children–Stephen, Alfred, Tina Papetti-Noll, and A.J.–entered the business and became vice presidents. They all knew that growth of their company had to be linked with teamwork, good people to get the job done, and most importantly, with good marketing. Papetti's did grow and became the industry leader in further processing. The most visible family member became a worldwide celebrity–Arthur Papetti.

A visit to Arthur's office is clearly an invitation into the inner chambers behind the dynasty. Behind the beautiful wooden desk sits a comfortable Arthur. His smile is friendly and encourages a frankness when talking about any issue, but one never forgets who is in control of the setting. Around the room is a visible demonstration of his passions. His family, as is typical among Italians, is first and foremost with the pictures on display. So too, his passion for waterfowl hunting with the mounted ducks on display around the room. His shotgun collection is among the finest anywhere, and Arthur enjoys talking about his hunting adventures. He is also passionate about moving forward in business. Even after retiring he maintains his consultancy with Michael Foods, Inc. and is active in providing advice and counsel to CEO Gregg Ostrander.

What's the story behind the Papetti name? Second generation, Alfred Papetti emigrated from Italy to America in the early 1900s and married Santina DeStefano. They started with a dairy farm, but as their family grew, they developed into the retail dairy and, later poultry business, in Elizabeth, NJ. They sold some eggs too, but the leakers and cracks were a problem. What to do with them? Those eggs were of no value so they simply threw them away. One day, Tony discovered a local bakery that purchased frozen eggs. To compete with their supplier, Papetti's started breaking the undergrades by hand, putting them in cans and freezing them. The profits from the sale of frozen whole egg were

surprising, so they started buying undergrades in
New Jersey. Pasta manufacturers appreciated the convenience of the Papetti product so the business grew. A new twist in the processing of egg products occurred when the manager from the pasta company telephoned about the labora-

tory results when the egg product was tested. The eggs tested "TMTC" (too many to count) in the aerobic plate tests. Since the Papettis were familiar with the dairy industry, the manager suggested pasteurizing the egg product like milk. No one was doing this on the East Coast, but the concept was sound. Arthur traveled to the Poultry & Egg Institute of America's Fact-Finding Conference in Kansas City in 1962 and talked to Kent Tomilson about an 1800 lb. per hour pasteurizer with a boiler for $12,000. When he returned home, the Papettis held a board meeting at the kitchen table. This was where the family made all of their important decisions. There was much discussion by the family over the purchase of equipment not used by others in the egg business, yet the concept was understood. The purchase was made. Papetti's started pasteurizing egg product. It turned out to be a great decision because shortly afterwards, the government issued a regulation that any egg product crossing the state line had to be pasteurized. Papetti's had the edge and was selling pasteurized product.

Papetti's continued to grow, but without the help of the local banks. Building a plant to process shell eggs into egg product was unheard of, so Tony oversaw all the expansion projects, piece by piece. After Arthur married Barbara, the cash they received from the gifts at their wedding amounted to $35,000. Arthur kept $500 for themselves and used the remainder to finance the plant construction, with Tony contributing his life savings as well. Santina handled the accounting so she called all the vendors to inform them of their new pay schedule of 5-6 weeks instead of the usual 14 days. The reliability of Papetti's previous payment history allowed them the extra time by their vendors.

A new problem popped up; the disposal of the shells. The local garbage collectors were getting an increased volume of shells and they didn't like the smell. The Papettis sought to dispose of the shells in the local landfill themselves, but Alfred had to get permission from those who organized the garbage collection in that area. The authorities said as  long as the Papettis only picked up shells, they had no objections. Arthur drove the truck twice daily, once at 6 a.m. and then again at 4 p.m. His coveralls fit over his clothes, which he wore to work after driving the truck to the dump. By 1968 Papetti's Hygrade Egg Products was up and running. Again, they were ahead of their time, for the federal government issued the Egg Products Inspection Act calling for mandatory inspection. Papetti's Hygrade Egg Products was ready.

Growth could only occur when there were markets for the product and the right team to execute. Many thanks to Mike Meloro of Farbest Tallman, Gus Minkin and Joe Weisman of Nearby Egg, along with Shep Shaff, Bob Kellert and Richard Broad of Bender Goodman Company for making Papetti's #1 in industrial sales of egg products in the United States. Papetti's started exhibiting their products at foodservice shows demonstrating a pathogen-free product that reduces labor and is more convenient than buying shell eggs. When buyers saw and sampled the taste of these new products, Papetti's sales soared.

The combination of knowledge from A.J. and Al, with the loyalty and drive from production managers John Burke, George Pigna, Ted Polny, and hard-cooked division's John Gill, Papetti's was producing egg products second to none. With an "eggstra-ordinary" research and development genius of Al Knipper on board, Papetti's was able create cutting edge products in the egg industry. In order to accomplish being Number One, Papetti's had their own "dream team," a sales force headed up by the dynamic duo of Stephen and Tina Papetti that swept the country by storm! Their goal was to become #1 in the world and remain there...and they did! With the help of key players Larry Rubin, "The Egg Baron of Norton," Vicky Wass, better known as "Eggatha", Craig Elliot, Bill Wagner, John Brommer, Spike and George Gavris, no customer or territory was left untouched. They were truly dedicated and continually strived for "egg-cellence."

Much gratitude goes to Al Wenger and Barry Shaw of Wenger Feed and to Toby Catherman to help maintain a steady supply of eggs. Arthur and Tony co-owned about 50% of the layers. They were producing product from more than 13 million layers from Maine to Ohio, the Carolinas, Georgia and Alabama, but they needed the assurance of a steady supply of product 52 weeks of the year. With the growing demand, more processing facilities needed to become part of Papetti's. They purchased Quaker State Farms, which was managed by Toby Catherman, who soon became the company's main procurer of shell eggs. Egg Specialties, Holton Foods and Monark Egg Corporation were also purchased by the Company. The West Coast had product needs, so Papetti's put in a new plant, Papetti's of Iowa, in a joint venture with Tom Rechsteiner. The Midwest had the eggs and the processed product could easily be transported to California. Now Papetti's was able to produce dried, frozen, liquid and whatever product blend their customers wanted coast to coast. They were selling various formulations, mixtures and package types to ice cream manufacturers, large bakeries and mayonnaise manufacturers. The company philosophy on production and marketing was summed up by Arthur Papetti. He said "You have to be market-driven and not production-driven. You have to make sure you have a market before you produce the product. Papetti's has always created a market and then increased production."

It is not just the author of this book who believes in the greatness of Arthur Papetti and his family. Look at the other biographies of this book. The one name that is mentioned more than any other, regardless of where you are in the world, is Arthur Papetti. As Arthur would say, "You are only as good as the people around you." That's the best advice for the incoming generation of egg people. First build the team, and then you can build a dynasty. And that's no yolk!

AL POPE

Some called him a "visionary," others called him "flexible," some say "innovative," but after 30 plus years leading the nation's egg cooperative/association, Al Pope still emphasizes the importance of unity within the industry. It's this "unity" that inspired Al to be the driving force behind the creation of the American Egg Board, the Egg Nutrition Center, and United Egg Association. The Europeans credit Al with motivating enthusiasm and support for the International Egg Commission, which now boasts membership on every continent of the world.

Before coming to the egg industry in 1974 as general manager of United Egg Producers, Al was affiliated with associations representing the wholesale grocery cooperatives. In 1974 there were thousands of egg producers, but today the numbers have dwindled down to about 200. Egg processors have also seen the consolidations to where 30 companies or so are processing the 30+% of all the shell eggs produced in the U.S. Al has viewed his position of President at UEP as a facilitator of the industry issues. He often amused his staff by pretending to be stirring a big stick in a pot and saying his job was to "stir up action" on those most pressing issues like market economics, animal welfare, food safety and government relations. When USDA/AMS Poultry Chief Conner Kennett approached Al in 1983 about organizing the egg processors, he thought he would be jumping into that pot he was stirring. The idea of organizing the egg processors and egg producers was about as welcome as a Republican at the Democratic National Headquarters. Al pressed forward with the idea, especially with the likes of those in the leadership of the egg processors–Vic Henningsen, Art Papetti, Dan Gardner, Len Ballas and Harold Cutler. Al helped both groups to recognize that other than the buyer-seller disagreements, there were many common issues among them and that the actions of one group should not negatively impact on the other. Forming the association also provided the mechanism for EggPAC, the political action committee which helped strengthen the government relations activities of both groups in Washington, D.C. Over the 30 years, the industry has seen many changes, including processors starting production facilities, and the advent of in-line processing. Al dreams that the role of the egg in the consumer's diet will advance more dramatically in the future as a functional food with an increasing role in the diets of an aging population.

Al describes his most memorable moment in 1990 when then chairman of UEP Dan Gardner informed him, in Dan's usual diplomatic style, "Pope - if this isn't straightened out and corrected by the first of the year, you will be replaced." Al understood that message and pulled out the stops to make the corrections before the first of the year. Dan and Al became great friends, and remained friends right up to Dan's death.

Al is proud of the many accomplishments during his 30+ years in the industry, but credits his staff as his proudest accomplishment. He noted that his staff was proactive, enthusiastic, loyal and respectful of the industry they served. Certainly, Al set the example for his staff to follow. He and his wife Penny are also very proud of their three children and six grandchildren.

Lou Raffel,

President of the American Egg Board

Chicago, Illinois

Modesty is a rare quality among chief executives, but in Lou Raffel it underscores his management style. The success of the American Egg Board since its inception in 1974 (officially active in 1976), and its continued success under Lou's leadership is tribute to his organizational skills, accomplishments in achieving program success, and in building producer support for the advertising and promotion programs that have carried the egg industry through good years and bad.

Yet, Lou says his heroes are the guys who had the vision to start

AEB – pioneers in the industry like John Wallace, Jerry Bookey, Fred Adams, Mike Hirth, Henk Wentink, Connor Kennett–unselfish guys who started AEB because they cared about the industry and wanted to make it better for everybody. We have to include Lou Raffel in that list, because ship builders show innovation and ingenuity, but the ship's captain steers that ship through the stormy seas. Lou has been an excellent captain at the helm of the American Egg Board these past 30 years.

AEB didn't follow the pattern of another promotion board. It led the way and was a model for the Beef Board, Pork Board, Dairy Board and others that followed. The law that established AEB said its mission is to increase the demand for eggs, egg products, and spent fowl. In the beginning, it was basically a shell egg organization. No one could have anticipated the tremendous growth of the egg products industry, and the integration of producers and processors and the synergistic impact it would have.

Recognizing the growing importance of further processed products, AEB instituted a major Further Processed Products program spearheaded by AEB's Senior Vice President Joanne Ivy. This program is applauded by the egg products industry as more and more ingredient manufacturers and others see where to find their specific needs. Lou's background was assistant public relations director of the American Meat Institute, public relations director of National Dairy Council, vice president of Armour & Co, and its parent company, Greyhound Corp. Having experience in meat and dairy was a perfect fit and a chance to head a brand new organization represented an exciting new challenge. Lou considers himself fortunate to have known and worked with many of the leaders of both the shell egg and egg products industries.

Lou says with fondness that Art Papetti paid AEB one of its greatest honors when, at the time of his retirement, he and his family presented AEB with a grant of $50,000 to help promote further processed egg products.

Among AEB's greatest achievements is the steady improvement

in consumer attitudes towards eggs. It was important to understand early on that AEB could not make the cholesterol scare go away without sound science to back up the messages. It was a slow process to get the research, but it is what paid off in the end. Without the science to back it up, AEB had very little credibility with either consumers or the scientific community.

The Incredible Edible Egg is one of the best food slogans ever created. Lou doesn't take the credit for inventing it, but he recognized its value from the beginning and has made sure it remained an important part of all AEB's advertising and promotion. That goes for Lou also! The industry recognized Lou's value as president of the American Egg Board and the industry has made sure that he remains an important part of all of AEB's advertising and promotion. Thank you, Lou. Everyone in the egg industry and egg products industry salutes the efforts and accomplishments you have made through the AEB.

TOM RECHSTEINER

On his wife's birthday, February 18, 1991, Tom Rechsteiner broke the first egg at the 84,000 square feet egg processing plant in Lennox, Iowa. It was the largest plant at that time. Tom and his wife Toni were partners with Arthur and Tony Papetti when the plant opened and that relationship continued to grow right through the company's sale to Michael Foods in 1997, and Tom's working for Michael's as VP of Industrial and Export Sales. He planned on retiring at the end of 2005. Toni has already taken her name off the door at the plant, but not before retiring as public relations director in 1999.

Tom grew up in the egg business. In his high school days, he started working for the Sheridan Egg Company making egg cases and cleaning floors. He later moved into a fulltime position cartoning eggs for retail, running a farm egg route, shift supervisor, then plant manager. In 1983 Tom and Toni bought the business. They upgraded operations to include the processing and packaging of liquid and frozen egg products. In 1988 they joined forces with the Papetti's with a 50% partnership. In addition to Toni's involvement in the business, their two children, Shellie and David, also spent time at the plant.

Tom recalls how production and processing of eggs has changed so dramatically over the years. In the 60s, he recalls that most every farmer had a few chickens. A major egg production facility then was 500 birds. That has grown to multi-million chickens at a single farm providing shell eggs for offline breakers as well as the inline complexes. Tom foresees continuing growth with more consolidations in the future. He also proudly exclaims how continuing growth in egg consumption will come with the newer products being developed, including those by Michael Foods. Tom says the industry needs to grow in developing a better procurement and marketing system. The new generations of people in the egg business need to learn and implement these better systems, and work hard. He says the end results are rewarding and satisfying if they work for them.

People who have had a direct impact on Tom's career in the egg business include Jerry Sheridan, who started him off in the business, Arthur and Tony Papetti for their unblinking vision to always welcome a challenge; Wes Horn for helping establish business contacts along with his technical support in designing their facility, and Sid Weksler for being a good friend to everyone in the business.

DAVE RETTIG

Rembrandt Enterprises

"Rembrandt is also an egg form!"

Dave Rettig is a man with a project. He developed an idea of putting laying hens into a complex that then ran the eggs into breaking machines and became the low cost producer. He is the son of a long time eggman, Darrel Rettig, who has had layers and distributed eggs for many years. But where Dave differed from many eggmen of the past was his ability to explain what he envisioned.

Dave has had a career that ranges from working as an aide to

Senator Bob Dole's campaign, to designing a brand of ice cream and setting up a system to distribute it. But his desires to get into the egg business led to him finding partners and building a modern production facility in Rembrandt, Iowa with 4 million layers, which has been one of the early models now being done by other companies.

Dave and his wife Jennifer live in Spirit Lake, Iowa and his hobbies include running and being a tester of the great food his wife makes for her catering/restaurant business. Our industry will watch for his future projects as he continues to look at the egg business in a different way: his style tells you that innovation will follow, as he hasn't taken the normal path to developing an egg business.

GOODWIN (GOODIE) SONSTEGARD

Sonstegard Foods

The fur industry has had a very successful ad campaign for many years entitled, "What Becomes A Legend Most," and in remembering eggman Goodie Sonstegard, it seems appropriate to describe him as a legendary eggman and mink rancher.

Goodie was born February 4, 1913 in Kandlyohl County, Minnesota to Peter Olaf and Selma Sonstegard, who were farmers and descendents of immigrants from Norway. He graduated from the University of Minnesota with a B.S. in animal husbandry and agricultural economics, and married Josephine in 1940. He was an owner and operator of cheese factories near Austin, Pipestone and Belgrade, Minnesota in the early 1940s and

then became a USDA inspector of dried and frozen eggs. From 1943 to 1972 he was a partner and the manager of Marshall Produce Company. His partner was Julius Weiner and there are many stories about the egg trading that this company did, ultimately becoming the largest egg products manufacturer in the United States at that time. He and Julius were also large growers of mink.

In 1972 Goodie left Marshall to found Sonstegard Foods with his son, Phil. Goodie was a very well known figure in the U.S. egg industry and active in many organizations. If you went to any meeting in the egg industry you would see Goodie, often wearing a very stylish fur coat, which made him stand out with his head of white hair in the crowd. Goodie was a legend also for his friendliness and his assistance to younger egg people coming into the industry. Dean Hughson remembers meeting Goodie and Phil at a mink meeting for the first time and Goodie being the first person to sit down and tell him the history of the egg industry; even with competitors he was friendly and his sense of humor was immense.

Goodie was quite active on a national basis in agricultural issues, serving as an advisor to Senator Hubert Humphrey and Vice President Walter Mondale. He was active in the National Grange and numerous other agricultural groups. He was also interested in farming and, like his ancestors, farmed. Goodie was also an investor in a gold mine and enjoyed traveling to Canada to check on it. He was very well read in what was happening on a national and international basis in agriculture. Under Goodie and Phil's stewardship, Sonstegard Foods grew to be one of the largest egg products companies in the United States with sales worldwide. His vision continues to this day.

Goodie died 5-8-1988 and is survived by sons Dr. Phil Sonstegard and Dr. Louis Sonstegard and daughter Pamela McWilliams, their spouses, and 11 grandchildren.

Goodie truly is a legend in the egg industry and his leadership is missed.

Rudolf "Rudy" O. Schmid

Luchinger & Schmid

Kloten, Switzerland

With the skills of speaking fluently three languages (German, French, English, but he also speaks a fourth), Rudy Schmid still wishes he had learned more languages and wishes he had a degree in food engineering.

Rudy is well educated already, having both a law degree along with an MBA. As an egg trader in Switzerland and a processor of all sorts of egg products, Rudy sees the value of languages in international business relationships. He loves his work and says being an entrepreneur has many advantages. But getting to where he is today required a great deal of work. His family (his father, brother and a sister) were in the business as minority shareholders. Their main interest was money, while Rudy enjoyed the challenges of the work, so he bought out the shares from his family. Then he merged the company with a bigger competitor and became the market leader in Switzerland. That brought on additional challenges with two different cultures involved in management. Today, Rudy is the only shareholder and enjoys sales to supermarkets, caterers and restaurants. Some of the products he sells are an omelet mix and a liquid scrambled egg mix sold to retail. His customer base of 4,000 includes other products too, besides egg products. Switzerland is a country where chickens are not producing eggs in cages so they are net importers of eggs (50%).

Being involved in the International Egg Commission, and former chairman of the Egg Products International, Rudy had developed contacts with egg exporters from around the world. At the meetings Rudy and Jurgen Fuchs spent a great amount of time together. At other times you may even see the two of them landing by helicopter on some isolated mountain slope and then skiing that mountain.

Rudy's most memorable experience involved his first truckload of eggs. When he bought the eggs from "old man Stadil," Rudy realized he needed to delay the arrival of the eggs. When he made the telephone call, Mr. Stadil informed him that in the egg business a man's word was his bond. Since Rudy had originally said he wanted the eggs, he was going to get them and that's it–a lesson Rudy never forgot about working with professionals in egg trading.

Today, Rudy believes in making things happen. There's no "probably" in his philosophy. Things don't probably happen. You must make them happen. Anyone who meets and gets to know Rudy will learn that he is one to make it happen.

What would Rudy recommend for the new generation of egg men entering the business? Work hard with the idea that your word is your word. Never give up! The smile on Rudy's face when you meet him tells you he never gave up.

PHIL SONSTEGARD

Sonstegard Foods

Sioux Falls, SD

One look at Phil Sonstegard and you can almost see the famous Civil War General William Tecumseh Sherman who pressed his army right through Atlanta and onto the sea at Savannah two days before Christmas in 1864. Both William Tecumseh Sherman and Phil Sonstegard have had difficult journeys. Both questioned if they could accomplish their assignments. Both demonstrated that determination and guts will get you through. Both succeeded. Here's Phil's story.

Thirty-two years ago, Phil Sonstegard bought an older plant for $100,000 with the terms of $10,000 per year payback for 10 years. Today he is operating five plants in four states and a layer complex, and is considered "a force to be reckoned with" in the egg products industry. Phil Sonstegard says he was "all guts, and no brains" when he started with the purchase of his plant in 1972 at Howard Lake, Minnesota, but having achieved a doctorate degree in veterinary medicine, along with his success and the growth of Sonstegard Foods, belies his claims. Even though his plants require a great amount of Phil's time, he still has time for his wife Jackie and seven children. He has taken the children to the IEC meetings on occasion. At the annual IEC conference in South Africa, the children got to see and appreciate the people and culture of South Africa while also meeting the egg products people from around the world. To this day he talks about the marvels of that particular experience and has gone global in his marketing efforts.

Phil worked alongside his father, Goodie, at Marshall Produce in Marshall, Minnesota. He operated the egg whites division. When the operation was purchased in Howard Lake, they lived in an apartment in the plant without any heat. The Minnesota winter temperatures can drop to 20 below at night (perhaps the "no brains" description actually fits). No one can argue that it wasn't "gutsy" to start that way. There weren't any egg breakers in Minnesota at the time so they had to buy all their liquid. To add to his difficulties, his vendors expected payment in cash. Still, Phil pressed on. He found a market in 6 oz. pouches through the National School Lunch Program. Bender Goodman also helped out by selling some of Phil's product.

His first expansion effort was the Estherville Foods plant in Iowa. He turned that facility into a state-of-the-art plant, adding a freezer and storage facility. The third plant he purchased was Supreme Egg in Sioux City, Iowa. The fourth facility was the egg breaking and frozen egg plant in Gainesville, Georgia and then the fifth was the breaking facility in Springdale, Arkansas. To make sure of a steady supply of raw materials, Phil also entered into the egg production side of the business and built a layer complex west of Okabogie, Iowa.

What changes has he seen that advanced the egg products industry? Phil has watched the consolidations occurring throughout, but the inline breaking and processing facilities were the real advances. As to Phil's most memorable experience, it goes back to the days of Howard Lake, getting started with no more than a dream and a loan, but today he can see how his hard work has paid off.

Bob Sparboe

He speaks softly, but his comments are complex and profound. In interviewing Bob Sparboe, Sparboe Companies, Litchfield, Minnesota, one's inquiries are met with thought-provoking questions from Bob. He's probing what's important to you while imparting his thoughts and perspectives. His final analysis from the exchange of information is translated into a way for Bob to look at life and business intrinsically. He espouses that achievement is what truly motivates people. Achievement is the "mother of motivation." In talking with Bob Sparboe you recognize quickly that he is passionate about people reaching their full potential. When his employees realize his passion for their personal success, they are motivated to accomplish the tasks at hand, and that propels Sparboe Companies to even greater accomplishments, as evidenced in industry statistics. Bob's formula for success is an inspiration to his employees and underscores his personal friendships, of which I am proud to be one.

Bob searches for usefulness in adversity and he searches for ways to draw positive energy and direction from it. That is how he started in the poultry and egg business, growing up in Iowa as the son of a hatchery man. He had a great home in which to grow. His father was able to impart leadership skills by osmosis. For example, Bob was never asked to mow the lawn by his father, he just knew it needed mowing and he did it. When obstacles or objectives were in sight, Bob confronted them as his father would. He confronted them as any leader would...head on, but using his head. His team of leaders in the Sparboe Companies has learned those leadership skills in the same way. Bob is very proud of company members and his face breaks into a wide smile when he talks about having the best production and marketing team in the industry.

As a youth, on hatch days, Bob was up at 4 a.m. to help pull off the hatch. While in high school, he continued to work 30 hours per week. In his formative years, Bob recalls how his father, Carl, would invite interesting guests to Sunday dinner. The Sunday mealtime conversations introduced Bob to people from all walks of life. In talking with people, Bob learned that everyone has dreams and ambitions. He was determined to learn to harvest energy and direction from the process of making his dreams come true. He recalls with fondness an acquaintance from Mississippi who made a chick delivery with him. His friend's name was Jim Costin. Jim asked Bob about some standing water in a field of corn. "Is that water an asset or a liability?" Bob answered by saying that was a stupid question. Jim responded that the water was whatever you wanted to make it. Dream solutions to perceived liabilities then seize the opportunities to make your dreams come true. Those who don't reach out for the opportunities are not achieving their true potential. We ourselves are frequently our worst enemies unless we manage through our frailties. Bob recalls that question and the lesson from Jim to this day.

    At the time of the Korean conflict, Bob was drafted into the Army. He graduated from the Infantry School at Fort Benning, Georgia, as a Second Lieutenant and served for a year in South Korea. Before returning from South Korea, he asked his father to sell him 10% of the family business. His father promptly answered stating, "that would not be in your best interest." But that was not a dead end for Bob. The marketing manager at Hy-Line Poultry Farms offered Bob an opportunity to distribute Hy-Line chicks. Before returning to the United States, Bob selected Litchfield as the home of what later become Sparboe Companies. During the first year of operation, egg prices fell from a war-economy-driven price of $.65 per dozen to $.16 per dozen. Bob transitioned into selling started pullets, resulting from unsold surpluses of chicks, finding much more profit in the started pullet business. Started pullet production quadrupled each year until 1966 when Marek's disease devastated the egg industry. The mortality rate was consistently so high that pullets could not be sold. Remaining pullets were put out in contract producer's facilities, thrusting the Sparboe Companies into the egg business. Much of the growth and new business development has been the Sparboe Companies constructive reaction to difficulties. The Sparboe Companies presently is one of the five largest egg producing companies in the United States, operating production and breaking facilities in three states.

One of his early activities in the US Egg Industry included Egg Clearinghouse, Inc. (ECI). His philosophy in life helped guide ECI to survive during some difficult years. ECI became strong because it handled its early challenges very well.

Sparboe Companies is global in its perspectives. The company sold more than 1.5 million cases of eggs into foreign markets during the last 12 months. Sparboe Companies will continue to ship shell eggs into those developing markets as opportunities arise.

Bob is married to Deanna and has three children, Garth Sparboe and Beth Schnell and Mark Sparboe. Beth remains working as a senior vice president of the Sparboe Companies in marketing and sales, and is currently serving as chairperson for the American Egg Board. Garth and Mark have branched out on their own, accepting the challenges of other endeavors.

When asked what Bob would recommend to the new generation of egg industry members, he said "to look and see the possibilities in your challenges. Take the long look and listen and hear." Bob Sparboe is one of a kind. His first question when this interview began was to determine what the reason is for writing this book. The answer is now obvious to anyone reading this story about Bob. Leaders like Bob Sparboe don't just happen with years of life. They happen because Bob made them happen. He's truly an inspiration to all.

The following is taken from Bob's annual 2005 New Year's card.

Making a Dream Come True

A dream is a vision of a wonderful possibility,
painted on a canvas of the dreamer's imagination.
To make a dream come true, one must believe in the
dream with heart and soul; the dreamer must –
—see the possibility in the dream.
—freely use the power of the dream.
—use obstacles as stepping stones.
—find usefulness in adversity.
—harvest energy and direction from the process of making the dream come true.

The dreamer must become one with the dream.
Bob Sparboe, 1/1/05
Epilogue: Sadly this was Bob's last interview as he died on October 8, 2005. He will be missed by us all.

STEVE STEWART

"It smells like money," said Steve Stewart as we walked through the inedible egg drying operation of ADF's Social Circle, Georgia three spray dryers and one evaporator. After 22 years of working with ADF in producing inedible egg powder for pet foods, Steve appreciates that the egg industry waste products can be revenue-generators for those with an imagination. It was Steve's responsibility to get the Social Circle plant built, staffed, and operational in the shortest time possible to fill production needs. He did just so, and they started drying inedible egg product February 28,1984 on an old box dryer cannibalized from some old plant in Nebraska. With the help of Bill Rey (ADF corporate engineer), Jim Hood (Specialty Manufacturing Company) and Steve, along with many others and after long hours, started turning out a product from the inedible of other plants. Steve has held positions with ADF as plant manager, Southern Division manager and vice president. When it comes to mentors, or just plain, good people, Steve says he's been very fortunate to be able to work for a man like Bill Darr all these years.

Steve started working summers at National Egg Products, Inc. (NEPCO) in Social Circle, Georgia in the summer of 1972. His first jobs were washing plastic egg flats, loading out 30 lb. tins of frozen egg product, and unloading cases and racks of breaking stock from trucks to the cooler. He worked for NEPCO part and full-time through 1983 while he finished high school and attended DeKalb Tech and DeKalb Community College. Steve held positions of receiving foreman, shell egg procurement assistant, transfer room manager and assistant production manager and learned quite a lot from Gib Grey, a real pioneer in the breaking industry, before leaving NEPCO to go to work for American Dehydrated Foods, Inc. in December of 1983. Steve was also active in United Egg Association, having served for years as the chairman of the Political Action Committee. His was a familiar face at the meetings, and a familiar voice when he called the egg products members asking for

their financial support in assisting the staff who worked in Washington, D.C.

Steve has been married for 28 years to his lovely wife Vicki and they have two wonderful daughters–Stephanie (25) and Rebecca (22) and one grandchild–Austin (4 months). Steve met Vicki when she was a secretary at NEPCO. Both her mother and father had worked in the poultry industry, Arbor Acres in Blairesville, Georgia and her father, Jay Groves, worked until retirement for NEPCO as maintenance manager. The egg products industry is truly glad to have folks like Steve Stewart and all the rest at ADF take their inedible egg liquid and turn it into a revenue source. When you wrinkle your nose walking through the plant, Steve smiles and says, "it smells like money to me."

ILYA SUSTER - From British Solder to

British Egg Products Industry

One lone Russian solder at his checkpoint on the road from Hamburg, Germany to Berlin stopped the column of Allied soldiers as they prepared to enter and occupy Berlin during WWII. Sergeant Ilya Suster, who spoke fluent Russian and German, got out of the jeep to explain to that lone Russian solder that the entire Allied forces were right behind him.

That lone solder had not been informed of the advancing Allied forces numbering into the tens of thousands of soldiers, so Ilya urged him to check with his commanding officer. Off that soldier went on his bicycle 8 kilometers to inquire if he should let the column of soldiers past his checkpoint. Of course, when he returned, the column advanced. As the driver of an armored personal carrier in WWII Sergeant Ilya Suster had been in many significant locations during the war. He was in Egypt with the Desert Rats after German General Romel was in retreat. He was at Normandy, France just over one and half months after the massive invasion by the Allied forces. He was also involved in the heavy Allied fighting at Salerno, Italy and then with the Allied forces entering Berlin. It was there that Ilya photographed General George Patton standing on the balcony with Field Marshall Shercoff. At 91 years of age, Ilya could remember that day and the events of the Second World War as if they occurred last year.

Ilya Suster was born in 1914 in Manchuria, China where his Latvian parents had traveled on business. Ilya's father worked with Samuel Behr in exporting shell eggs from China to Germany and England. Around 1909, Ilya's father discovered that shell eggs packed in rice husks would be preserved longer. Weather was also important. If the temperatures in Europe were cold, the hens there were not laying and this was an opportunity too good to pass up. The exporting of shell eggs from China was accomplished through "compradores," brokers who knew and understood the exporting business and whom the Chinese knew and trusted. The eggs were referred to as "penny eggs," as they were sold for one penny each to Sainsbury and others.

Samuel Behr played a significant role in shaping Ilya's future. Once a ship loaded with eggs for Europe sailed without necessary export certificates. The eggs were ready, so the ship left without the documents. Samuel Behr had not paid the Chinese since the ship sailed before completing all the arrangements, but he did return to pay his obligations to the Chinese. This experience taught Ilya a lesson he later carried thoughout his life. In 1926, Samuel Behr built "Kalteburg" (cold castle), a cold storage building for the eggs in Hamburg. It was the second-largest storage facility in Europe. With room enough for 150 million eggs, the facility was never completely filled. Every month the boxes of eggs in the cold storage facility had to be turned so that the yolks remained centered. Ilya entered the business after World War II, coming from the tomato business after importing tomato puree from Italy. The company then was called S. Behr and Matthews, and Ilya was appointed the sales director. Ilya did well working in sales, but found the job very difficult. He attributed much of difficulty to the managing director.

Ilya entered into the egg products industry in the mid-60s breaking and drying eggs. The name of the company was Londegg, and it was here he worked until he liquidated operations to retire. He sold eggs throughout Europe and to Bender Goodman and others in the United States.

When asked what Ilya would recommend to the new generation of egg products businessmen, Ilya said, "Don't," implying that the business of buying and trading eggs and egg products is getting more and more tricky. Samuel Behr helped him appreciate the importance of integrity to maintaining a good business relationship.

That is why Behr returned to China to pay off his obligations when the ship sailed without its export certificates. Ilya said a man's word was his contract and the need for long-worded contracts and attorneys was unnecessary then. But that has all changed now.

After our pleasant conversation, Ilya Suster got into a London taxi and returned to his wife, where they both live in the Northwestern part of London today. He perhaps can be described as a link to the history of the egg industry and the only person left who can describe the early egg trade personally.

Dennis Tyrrell

Estherville Foods

Dennis Tyrrell is perhaps one of the best known egg products people in the industry. He began his involvement in eggs working for an accounting firm in Minnesota which had long time eggman Goodie Sonstegard as a customer. Goodie hired Dennis to work for Marshall Foods in Marshall, Minnesota. Later, Dennis left Marshall to head to California and Egg City and DeCoster in Maine, but his involvement with the Sonstegard Family was not to end.

In 1976 Dennis assisted Sonstegard in taking over Estherville Foods in Estherville, Iowa and since then has built it into a major leader in egg products. For those in the Midwest Dennis is known for hard work and dedication to our industry and rarely being away from his desk. He thrives on the egg business. When asked about retirement Dennis said, "This is what I like to do and I have no intention to retire when I enjoy my work every day." He is a frequent participant in egg industry meetings and involved in purchasing many eggs and tankers of liquid eggs in the Midwest, besides his own large break.

Dennis and his wife Pat have three children. His two sons-in-law are involved in Dennis's farming operation– Annette and Tom Zebedee and Tina and Bruce Zebedee. They also have a son and daughter-in-law, Ken and Danette Tyrrell. Dennis and Pat have eight grandchildren.

FILIEP VAN BOSSTRAETEN

From the Air Force, to fish factory, to egg products producer, to egg processing equipment sales . . . these were the career steps for Filiep Van Bosstraeten leading up to general manager for Ovobel in Brugge, Belgium. After leaving the Belgian Air Force and marrying Yvonne in 1960, Filiep started working in a fish factory. Here he purchased ingredients for that company, including salted egg yolk from China in wooden barrels for the production of mayonnaise. His actual start in the egg products industry began with his first contract for salted egg yolk. He agreed to supply 20 tons monthly. Just one problem: Filiep had no equipment (he had prepared his sales samples in the kitchen sink). Within two weeks he created a mini-plant and with hard working women, breaking and separating eggs manually, he managed to deliver the product on time. This contract was the start of his career in egg products.

The creation of the European Union made it more difficult to import agricultural products from third countries due to the stricter health controls within the EU and higher levies. So, Filiep, along with a Belgian farmer, started the production of egg products in 1961. Initially it was a manual operation and they employed young women for breaking and separating egg yolk and egg whites. Egg yolks were mixed and salted (up to 15 %) mainly for mayonnaise manufacturers and egg white

was frozen, then sold to the bakery and meat industry. Before that beginning, the egg products industry was non-existent. Packing stations did make whole egg from their second quality eggs for local bakeries and so did the hatcheries from their incubator clears.

In the mid sixties they introduced a Dutch breaking machine "COLUMBUS" with a capacity of 6000 eggs per hour. Initially this machine could only produce whole egg. New technology was later developed providing the automatic separation of yolks and whites. From the Dutch producer of this breaking machine Filiep obtained the exclusive distribution rights for the equipment in all of Europe. They sold several hundred of these machines to egg processors, but the main customers were the bigger bakeries.

In the U.K. how they dealt with egg surpluses provided a good start into the sales of equipment. The "British Egg Marketing Board" (BEMB) operated a supply-management program for the egg industry (prior to UK joining the EU). All egg surpluses were broken (processed into whole egg) and frozen in BEMB- approved plants. The plants were Filiep's biggest customers. They included Croda, Export Packers, Frampton, Goldrei-Foucard, Greenall, Layton, LondEgg, Rannoch, Reich. Today, only Frampton's and Reich (now known as Deans Foods) are still in the business.

Pasteurization of egg products became compulsory in the late sixties. In 1967, with some Belgian producers, he made a tour in the USA and visited Seymour (Mr. Chamberlain) along with a number of egg processors. In 1972, as a delegate from the Belgian egg packer association, Filiep came to salvage about 70 container loads of Belgian eggs. He managed to recover the eggs and sold them to U.S. egg processors.

In partnership with Mr. De Meester, a Belgian egg producer, they built a modern egg processing plant, BELOVO in Bastogne, Belgium which became one of the most important egg processing plants in Europe. Simultaneously, Filiep also expanded in the egg processing equipment business and created OVOBEL, exclusively for selling expertise and equipment for the egg products industry. Filiep remained active in

Belovo as sales manager until the early eighties, when he decided to concentrate on Ovobel. His customer base was worldwide. Filiep had the exclusive distribution rights for the Coenraadts egg breaking machines and other equipment for the egg processing industry. He also was the exclusive agent in Europe for Food Engineering Services selling spray driers and special triple tube pasteurizers.

At Ovobel they are not only suppliers of equipment but also have a team of qualified engineers and programmers to design and build complete egg processing plants. Ovobel can even provide in-house plant managers to start up and run the plants as long as required by the clients. Among Filiep's accomplishments and contributions, he was instrumental in the development of the egg processing industry, from an archaic manual operation to the high tech, modern industry of today. With that modernization came new pressures of stricter regulations and higher quality requirements of the big end users. More specifically, he worked to see the creation of fresh liquid products with extended shelf life to which Ovobel contributed with the introduction of the triple tube pasteurizer from FES in Europe and the aseptic packaging. The introduction of the "AlbuMaster" on the Coenraadts breaking machine for the automatic separation of egg yolk and egg white using the latest optical scanning technology reduced the labor requirements considerably. He also played a major role in the creation of the Belgian egg processors association which became the Union of Belgian Egg Processors. He also organized the first meeting of the European Egg Processors Association, which today represents more than 90% of all processors in Europe.

Filiep participated in the activities of the International Egg Commission since the mid sixties and is universally acknowledged as among the most important people in the egg products industry. In 1999, the IEC presented him with the first ever "Denis Wellstead Memorial Trophy" as the International Egg Person of the year 1999. But Filiep likes to credit his many friends in the industry. These include alphabetically : Abreu (Argentina), Bouchier (Belgium), Coenraadts (Holland), Dean (UK), De Meester (Belgium), Enthoven (Holland), Ernst (Denmark), Frampton (UK), Fuchs (Germany), Gandolfi (Italy), Goede (Holland), Honum (Denmark), Imai (Japan), Justeau (France), Kallbergs (Sweden), Kathmann (Germany), Kemp (UK), Lionello (Italy), Manton

(UK), Mehrpol (Germany), Monaldi (Italy), Pohlmann (Germany), Rao (India), Schmid (Switzerland), Van Dijk (Holland), Van den Burg (Holland), Van deWiele (Belgium), Zacharias (Brazil). In the US, he lists as friends, Len Ballas, Chamberlain, Harold and Joel Cutler, Dan Gardner, Joanne Ivy, Vic Henningsen, Ken Klippen, Bob Sparboe, Art Papetti, Al Pope, Gene Gregory. In Canada, Hugh Wiebe and Vicki Canada and Jane and Brian Elsworth. In Australia his very good friend is Frank Pace. There certainly are many more and he apologizes to those friends in the industry he did not remember at the time of the interview.

For the new generation of egg men, what does Filiep recommend? Try to use as much as possible the experience of the older people in our business, coupled with the new technologies. Become members of the national and international associations and make friends in the industry. Learn languages, which enables direct contacts with your colleagues. And last, but it is very important–if you marry, find a partner who will support you in your work and who can accept your frequent absences.

Dr. Milton G. Waldbaum

A young Navy officer spent World War II in a blimp that was put high off of the shores of Brazil each day looking for Nazi submarines. Since he had lots of hours to think he seriously considered what his future would be. He had decided not to return to live in New York City or the family grocery business and would set off on his own adventure. His degree in poultry science from Cornell was good preparation for what lay ahead. He and his wife Mimi set off to work with his brother, Sidney, in Grand Island, Nebraska.

Sidney had a small breaking plant in the middle of Nebraska and was drying eggs. During the war there were many egg driers in areas like Nebraska to supply dried egg to the military but the industry was changing. Quickly Milt decided that he didn't want to work with his brother and he began thinking about his future. He had to go to an egg meeting in Sioux City, Iowa and he chartered a small airplane to take him there. While enroute, the plane iced up and had to land in a field in Northeast Nebraska. The pilot couldn't see that under the snow drifts sat a race horse track and the undercarriage of the plane was damaged. Milt and the pilot were not hurt but they had to go to a hotel since it would take some time for someone to come and get them on the crude roads of the day. There was no hotel in the town where the wreck occurred so they were taken to the next town, which was Wakefield, Nebraska. While in the hotel he was talking to local people and they told him about a chicken plant across the street that had gone broke and left local people unemployed. He ended up buying the plant and thus began the Milton G. Waldbaum Company in 1950.

Milt began with women hand grading eggs and also breaking eggs. They also ran routes throughout the area picking up eggs from small producers and giving trading stamps as premiums. The eggs and frozen eggs were packed off and sent to grocery stores and bakeries on the East Coast. The railroad actually came through the middle of the plant and it required the 'hand breaking line' to be disassembled each night so that the train could pass through the site. As Milt needed some help he brought in two relatives of his and Mimi's family: Dan Gardner and David Brown. His first employee was a young local man, Don Paulsen, who at age 15 would drive Milt's car with a small trailer to haul off the egg shells. Milt and Mimi began their family and adopted Susan. But Milt's life still lacked satisfaction in his career and after talking about it with a few people, he decided to go to medical school. David Brown had health issues and left the company to move to California and Dan Gardner remained to become Milt's partner and run the day to day activities of the company. Milt's ability to balance medical studies and still be involved in day to day activities of the egg company by telephone and visits was legendary. Milt and Mimi moved to Omaha, Nebraska, adopted two more children, Jerry and John, and after graduation from medical school Doc then established a successful medical practice. The egg company grew rapidly through his vision of where the food industry was going and through prudent management of the earnings of the company. With his ability to get financing, the company grew to be a market leader, producing shell eggs for the new 'supermarkets,' liquid, frozen, and dried eggs for food manufacturers and export. Doc knew his employees by name and loved to walk around in the plant greeting friends, many of whom had been with him since day one. As the company expanded it became apparent that they needed their own production and Doc's original degree came in handy as they started some of the first 'large complexes' of layers in the United States. The company's location in the Midwest was ideal for benefiting from the ample grain in the area.

Doc was a visionary in many ways about trends in food manufacturing and he and his partner, Dan, worked well together in expansion. But his love of medicine was a good balance for his life and when he would be going around in Omaha, people would stop him to thank him for his excellent care of a relative; he was probably better known as a doctor in Omaha than as an eggman.

Doc unfortunately grew ill in the mid 1980s and was forced to retire from medicine and the egg business. In 1989 he and his family sold the company and began the Milton G. Waldbaum Family Foundation which established scholarship programs for former employees children and continues to provide funds for charities. He was an eggman's eggman and is missed by his family, which has grown to include grandchildren Amber, David, and Sarah Waldbaum, Rachel, Josh, and Elizabeth Hughson, and Adam, Jared, and Matthew Waldbaum.

Hugh Wiebe

He's the quiet Canadian with a gentle disposition, but his energy in developing ideas and new companies reminds one of a grizzly bear who fearlessly charges forward to challenge any competitor or defend his territory. Hugh Wiebe is the gentle giant from the North and he has earned the respect and admiration of many in the egg products industry worldwide. His work and development with Lysozyme is testimony to his many accomplishments. This is his story.

John Hugh Wiebe was born in Steinbach, Manitoba on July 16, 1945, the same day as the first US atomic bomb was tested. Hugh began his career working with his father and brothers in the family agricultural business, Brookside Farms, which was an integrated egg laying and processing business based in Western Canada. In 1975, Hugh took over as president of Brookside, and under his leadership transformed the company into a successful international egg processing and trading company.

Hugh continued to nurture his passion for developing new ideas into commercial reality, and in 1977, while seeking other value-added egg products, he founded Brookside Foods Ltd., a company that today manufactures a complete line of chocolate confections and is a leader in its category of products in Canada with plants in Abbotsford and St. Hyacinthe, Quebec to cover the Eastern markets of Canada and USA. In addition to its world-renowned Chocolate Bowl Almonds and other confectionery products, Brookside Foods has introduced Fruit Chips to meet the demands of the market place.

In 1978, an alliance between Brookside Ltd. and Vanderpol's Eggs Ltd. was developed. This alliance allowed both companies more marketing and production strength in the Canadian and international markets. In 1993, Canadian Inovatech Inc. was formed, merging Canadian Lysozyme and Vanderpol's. This company in turn purchased their largest competitor in Canada, Export Packers' egg division. Canadian Inovatech grew both in Canada and internationally, becoming one of the largest suppliers of egg products to the Far East market.

In 1980, through his search to diversify eggs, Hugh developed another company, Canadian Lysozyme. This company developed the process of extracting an anti-bacterial product, Lysozyme, from the egg white. This new technology and process allowed Canadian Lysozyme to become one of the largest international suppliers of this product. In 1991, in order to service the European markets, an extraction facility was established in Zeewolde, Holland. Today, the operation processes a significant share of the Lysozyme in the world.

In the 90s Hugh established the nutrition division of Canadian

Inovatech Inc. A complete line of dairy and egg protein products was developed to fill the needs of emerging nutritional markets. Facilities were built in Canada, and joint ventures entered into in the United States and Europe for the production of these specialty nutritional products. A retail marketing company, Bioplex, was formed in 1999 to produce and sell nutritional products to the retail health food and nutritional marketplace.

In August 2002 the Egg division of Canadian Inovatech was sold to MFI Food Canada Ltd. and now operates as Inovatech Egg Products, leaving two divisions: BioProducts, now called Inovatech BioProducts, and Nutrition, now Vitalus Nutrition Inc. Inovatech BioProducts is a leader in the development of biologically active products (lysozyme and proteases) that contribute to health and well being. Inovatech BioProducts has offices and production facilities in Canada and Netherlands. Vitalus Nutrition Inc's products are dairy-based in nature and are unique for their value added nutrition and functionality. Vitalus has offices and production facilities in Canada, United States, Argentina, and the Netherlands.

Today, Hugh remains very busy in his various roles. He is president of Canadian Inovatech & Inovatech BioProducts, chairman and CEO of Vitalus Nutrition Inc, chairman of the board for Brookside Foods Ltd. and advisor to Inovatech Egg Products. In his limited spare time he does try to find chances to enjoy cruising the islands of Washington State and British Columbia aboard his boat, the Ova Due. Hugh has five siblings and two children—a son and daughter. Jason Wiebe recently married a lovely lady named Shauna and they are settling into their new home. Sharolyn Wiebe married Brian 10 years ago. Hugh patiently waits for grandchildren to carry on his legacy.

Vladimir Zacharius - Brazil

He finished his University degree in business and was working in his father's tire company around 1972 in Brazil. The economy was growing and there were a lot of new opportunities for those who wanted to start a new business. Vladimir joined with two friends from the University, Paulo Bonadia and Nelson Scuracchio, and they started in the egg industry business. Where did the idea to go into eggs come from? It was Paulo Bonadia whose family were traditional shell egg dealers. Vladimir thought the idea of selling one egg to two clients, the yolk and the white client, simply incredible. In November 1974 they started Sohovos. That was the beginning of the egg industry in South America.

Vladimir used to say that the egg business in Brazil is 10-15 years behind the chicken meat industry. So he expects acquisitions in the next few years. He expects to see more investments in R&D, more added value, not only as a food resource but also as raw material. The first time that he traveled abroad in 1976 was to visit Seymour's plant in Topeka, Kansas. After that he has made more than 50 trips because of the egg business.

Vladimir has scaled back in his time with the company while his son, Rodrigo Zacharias, and Nelson's son, Nelson Neto, are in charge of the company that has capacity to break 400 cases per hour.

As to new innovations, Vladimir notes the extended shelf life and the increase of the new uses and applications. Vladimir also noted the decrease of the commercial barriers and an international quality standard agreement allowing more people in the world to enjoy egg products with better quality and cheaper prices.

Vladimir recalls many friends in the egg business. He says he would do it all over again. He credits the international upgrading of his company when they joined the IEC. Vladimir serves as vice president with the ABIA (food industry association).

Mark Campbell

In early American history, those enterprising and energetic young men seeking fame and fortune would clutch hold of the inspiring words, "Go West, Young Man, Go West." That's what Mark Campbell did to claim his fame and fortune in the egg products business. Mark started his career in an egg grading plant in Quakertown, Pennsylvania. He soon moved on to The Olson Egg Products Plant in downtown Philadelphia, Pennsylvania. It was a small plant located in a very tough area, close to the Philadelphia Cutler Plant. This business was challenging for a young 24 year old learning the egg products business. He had the education; a Masters Degress in Economics from Utah State University. But he soon received an advanced education from the Cutler's and Papetti's people, who taught him more about the egg products business than could be learned from books.

Within a year the Olson Egg Products Plant closed the breaking operation and Mark moved West..on to Utah for some shell egg management experience. This assignment in Utah lasted about a year before a terrible cerebral accident took the life of the Olson's California egg breaking plant manager.

The call to "Go West" was sounded and Mark spent the next 10 years working in the Olson organization, always working hard to keep involved on the small Olson Lahabra egg breaking operation. Mark recognized the small niche market in egg products. It was very successful and Mark clutched hold of his future in egg products.

By 1983 Mark was assistant to the President of Olson Farms. Olson sold the Southern California business to Harry Eisen of Norco Ranch. Mark sought out advancement and moved on to Packers Cold Storage as Vice President of Operations until the untimely death of Chet Hicks at Norco's egg product operation. This would be the third time an unfortunate death had drawn Mark back into the egg breaking business.

In 1997 Norco merged their egg product business with Moark Egg products as Moark had purchased the Wecksler family business in Vernon, California. Mark found his "fame and fortune" in a niche market. He credits the success to hard work and good leadership with Doug Austin and presently Carl Forsage at the helm, and his wife Leesa supporting him and working in customer service at Norco.

In looking back, Mark noted the biggest changes in the egg products business are, of course, in-line breaking, extended shelf life and the pre-cooked egg. Of the three, Mark looks to the precooked egg as the future for egg products. He also foresees in the future more government regulation and production control though environmental issues, and consolidation in the industry with three major processors and ten niche players. He also feels that for the egg products business to grow there is a need to have the technology to create better pre-cooked items that reconstitute well.

The most memorable thing for Mark in his experiences is the fact that the real enterprising people in the egg products business were hooked on "MBWA," that is, "Management By Walking Around." They would "see for themselves" what was going on and what needed to be done. Just his exposure to this driven group is an exceptional experience, he says.

Mark had a mentor at Olson Farms in Gil Cochran, who spent years teaching him to market eggs. In addition, Arthur Papetti was always giving Mark advice. Mark also learned much working under Harry Eisen. Indeed, Mark worked with some of the great ones in the business. He listened, he learned and he accomplished.

"Go West, Young Man, Go West." Mark did that, but he carried the experiences and wisdom of great men like Gil Cochran, Arthur Papetti and Harry Eisen. The end result is Mark Campbell is listed among the great ones in the egg products industry.

Prologue by ARTHUR PAPETTI

I have spent a lifetime in the egg products business, and loved every minute of it. The experiences, the business deals we made with others, the travels to other lands to learn how they operate their egg products plants, are stories each in their own that I have shared with my children, their children and others. When I tell one of these stories, the audience invariably asks for more. It occurred to me one day, people I have known for decades in this business also have stories they are sharing, and their children and grandchildren are asking for more too. Why not make a collection of these stories and
publish it in a book?

Better yet, why not write a biography of the storytellers along

with their stories to share with everyone? That is when I shared my idea with Dean Hughson and Ken Klippen, two industry consultants who know the people in the industry, and have the drive to collect and publish the stories. So, here is the biography, "It Started With An Egg." Every effort was made to reach out to the egg products industry leaders of today and days gone by to include them in this book. Now, when I share my stories with my grandchildren, I can take the book off the shelf and read other stories too. This is a great industry and if I had to do it all over again, I would in a minute! With the book, I will continue to relive my "eggsperiences" and enjoy my friends and associates' memories as well.

ARTHUR PAPETTI